C-892 CAREER EXAMINATION SERIES

This is your
PASSBOOK for...

Welder

Test Preparation Study Guide
Questions & Answers

COPYRIGHT NOTICE

This book is SOLELY intended for, is sold ONLY to, and its use is RESTRICTED to individual, bona fide applicants or candidates who qualify by virtue of having seriously filed applications for appropriate license, certificate, professional and/or promotional advancement, higher school matriculation, scholarship, or other legitimate requirements of education and/or governmental authorities.

This book is NOT intended for use, class instruction, tutoring, training, duplication, copying, reprinting, excerption, or adaptation, etc., by:

1) Other publishers
2) Proprietors and/or Instructors of "Coaching" and/or Preparatory Courses
3) Personnel and/or Training Divisions of commercial, industrial, and governmental organizations
4) Schools, colleges, or universities and/or their departments and staffs, including teachers and other personnel
5) Testing Agencies or Bureaus
6) Study groups which seek by the purchase of a single volume to copy and/or duplicate and/or adapt this material for use by the group as a whole without having purchased individual volumes for each of the members of the group
7) Et al.

Such persons would be in violation of appropriate Federal and State statutes.

PROVISION OF LICENSING AGREEMENTS – Recognized educational, commercial, industrial, and governmental institutions and organizations, and others legitimately engaged in educational pursuits, including training, testing, and measurement activities, may address request for a licensing agreement to the copyright owners, who will determine whether, and under what conditions, including fees and charges, the materials in this book may be used them. In other words, a licensing facility exists for the legitimate use of the material in this book on other than an individual basis. However, it is asseverated and affirmed here that the material in this book CANNOT be used without the receipt of the express permission of such a licensing agreement from the Publishers. Inquiries re licensing should be addressed to the company, attention rights and permissions department.

All rights reserved, including the right of reproduction in whole or in part, in any form or by any means, electronic or mechanical, including photocopying, recording, or by any information storage and retrieval system, without permission in writing from the Publisher.

Copyright © 2025 by
National Learning Corporation

212 Michael Drive, Syosset, NY 11791
(516) 921-8888 • www.passbooks.com
E-mail: info@passbooks.com

PASSBOOK® SERIES

THE *PASSBOOK® SERIES* has been created to prepare applicants and candidates for the ultimate academic battlefield – the examination room.

At some time in our lives, each and every one of us may be required to take an examination – for validation, matriculation, admission, qualification, registration, certification, or licensure.

Based on the assumption that every applicant or candidate has met the basic formal educational standards, has taken the required number of courses, and read the necessary texts, the *PASSBOOK® SERIES* furnishes the one special preparation which may assure passing with confidence, instead of failing with insecurity. Examination questions – together with answers – are furnished as the basic vehicle for study so that the mysteries of the examination and its compounding difficulties may be eliminated or diminished by a sure method.

This book is meant to help you pass your examination provided that you qualify and are serious in your objective.

The entire field is reviewed through the huge store of content information which is succinctly presented through a provocative and challenging approach – the question-and-answer method.

A climate of success is established by furnishing the correct answers at the end of each test.

You soon learn to recognize types of questions, forms of questions, and patterns of questioning. You may even begin to anticipate expected outcomes.

You perceive that many questions are repeated or adapted so that you can gain acute insights, which may enable you to score many sure points.

You learn how to confront new questions, or types of questions, and to attack them confidently and work out the correct answers.

You note objectives and emphases, and recognize pitfalls and dangers, so that you may make positive educational adjustments.

Moreover, you are kept fully informed in relation to new concepts, methods, practices, and directions in the field.

You discover that you are actually taking the examination all the time: you are preparing for the examination by "taking" an examination, not by reading extraneous and/or supererogatory textbooks.

In short, this PASSBOOK®, used directedly, should be an important factor in helping you to pass your test.

WELDER

JOB DESCRIPTION
Under supervision, does electric arc and oxy-acetylene welding in all positions on both light and heavy material so as to maintain the proper size, contour, fusion, penetration and strength of welds and to prevent undercut, overlap and slag inclusions in welds; performs related work.

EXAMPLES OF TYPICAL TASKS
Reads and works from blueprints, sketches and working drawings. Properly uses the various types of welding rods and machines. Pre-heats and cleans metals. Lays out, cuts and fits materials for welding. Welds machinery and-equipment. Brazes various non-ferrous metals. Brushes and grinds welds.

SCOPE OF EXAMINATION
The written examination will be of the multiple-choice type and will contain questions relating to principles and practices of welding and related fields.
In the practical test, candidates will be required to make specimen welds depending on the classification selected. Candidates will also be required to demonstrate their ability to read and write English.

HOW TO TAKE A TEST

I. YOU MUST PASS AN EXAMINATION

A. *WHAT EVERY CANDIDATE SHOULD KNOW*

Examination applicants often ask us for help in preparing for the written test. What can I study in advance? What kinds of questions will be asked? How will the test be given? How will the papers be graded?

As an applicant for a civil service examination, you may be wondering about some of these things. Our purpose here is to suggest effective methods of advance study and to describe civil service examinations.

Your chances for success on this examination can be increased if you know how to prepare. Those "pre-examination jitters" can be reduced if you know what to expect. You can even experience an adventure in good citizenship if you know why civil service exams are given.

B. *WHY ARE CIVIL SERVICE EXAMINATIONS GIVEN?*

Civil service examinations are important to you in two ways. As a citizen, you want public jobs filled by employees who know how to do their work. As a job seeker, you want a fair chance to compete for that job on an equal footing with other candidates. The best-known means of accomplishing this two-fold goal is the competitive examination.

Exams are widely publicized throughout the nation. They may be administered for jobs in federal, state, city, municipal, town or village governments or agencies.

Any citizen may apply, with some limitations, such as the age or residence of applicants. Your experience and education may be reviewed to see whether you meet the requirements for the particular examination. When these requirements exist, they are reasonable and applied consistently to all applicants. Thus, a competitive examination may cause you some uneasiness now, but it is your privilege and safeguard.

C. *HOW ARE CIVIL SERVICE EXAMS DEVELOPED?*

Examinations are carefully written by trained technicians who are specialists in the field known as "psychological measurement," in consultation with recognized authorities in the field of work that the test will cover. These experts recommend the subject matter areas or skills to be tested; only those knowledges or skills important to your success on the job are included. The most reliable books and source materials available are used as references. Together, the experts and technicians judge the difficulty level of the questions.

Test technicians know how to phrase questions so that the problem is clearly stated. Their ethics do not permit "trick" or "catch" questions. Questions may have been tried out on sample groups, or subjected to statistical analysis, to determine their usefulness.

Written tests are often used in combination with performance tests, ratings of training and experience, and oral interviews. All of these measures combine to form the best-known means of finding the right person for the right job.

II. HOW TO PASS THE WRITTEN TEST

A. NATURE OF THE EXAMINATION

To prepare intelligently for civil service examinations, you should know how they differ from school examinations you have taken. In school you were assigned certain definite pages to read or subjects to cover. The examination questions were quite detailed and usually emphasized memory. Civil service exams, on the other hand, try to discover your present ability to perform the duties of a position, plus your potentiality to learn these duties. In other words, a civil service exam attempts to predict how successful you will be. Questions cover such a broad area that they cannot be as minute and detailed as school exam questions.

In the public service similar kinds of work, or positions, are grouped together in one "class." This process is known as *position-classification*. All the positions in a class are paid according to the salary range for that class. One class title covers all of these positions, and they are all tested by the same examination.

B. FOUR BASIC STEPS

1) Study the announcement

How, then, can you know what subjects to study? Our best answer is: "Learn as much as possible about the class of positions for which you've applied." The exam will test the knowledge, skills and abilities needed to do the work.

Your most valuable source of information about the position you want is the official exam announcement. This announcement lists the training and experience qualifications. Check these standards and apply only if you come reasonably close to meeting them.

The brief description of the position in the examination announcement offers some clues to the subjects which will be tested. Think about the job itself. Review the duties in your mind. Can you perform them, or are there some in which you are rusty? Fill in the blank spots in your preparation.

Many jurisdictions preview the written test in the exam announcement by including a section called "Knowledge and Abilities Required," "Scope of the Examination," or some similar heading. Here you will find out specifically what fields will be tested.

2) Review your own background

Once you learn in general what the position is all about, and what you need to know to do the work, ask yourself which subjects you already know fairly well and which need improvement. You may wonder whether to concentrate on improving your strong areas or on building some background in your fields of weakness. When the announcement has specified "some knowledge" or "considerable knowledge," or has used adjectives like "beginning principles of…" or "advanced … methods," you can get a clue as to the number and difficulty of questions to be asked in any given field. More questions, and hence broader coverage, would be included for those subjects which are more important in the work. Now weigh your strengths and weaknesses against the job requirements and prepare accordingly.

3) Determine the level of the position

Another way to tell how intensively you should prepare is to understand the level of the job for which you are applying. Is it the entering level? In other words, is this the position in which beginners in a field of work are hired? Or is it an intermediate or advanced level? Sometimes this is indicated by such words as "Junior" or "Senior" in the class title. Other jurisdictions use Roman numerals to designate the level – Clerk I, Clerk II, for example. The word "Supervisor" sometimes appears in the title. If the level is not indicated by the title, check the description of duties. Will you be working under very close supervision, or will you have responsibility for independent decisions in this work?

4) Choose appropriate study materials

Now that you know the subjects to be examined and the relative amount of each subject to be covered, you can choose suitable study materials. For beginning level jobs, or even advanced ones, if you have a pronounced weakness in some aspect of your training, read a modern, standard textbook in that field. Be sure it is up to date and has general coverage. Such books are normally available at your library, and the librarian will be glad to help you locate one. For entry-level positions, questions of appropriate difficulty are chosen – neither highly advanced questions, nor those too simple. Such questions require careful thought but not advanced training.

If the position for which you are applying is technical or advanced, you will read more advanced, specialized material. If you are already familiar with the basic principles of your field, elementary textbooks would waste your time. Concentrate on advanced textbooks and technical periodicals. Think through the concepts and review difficult problems in your field.

These are all general sources. You can get more ideas on your own initiative, following these leads. For example, training manuals and publications of the government agency which employs workers in your field can be useful, particularly for technical and professional positions. A letter or visit to the government department involved may result in more specific study suggestions, and certainly will provide you with a more definite idea of the exact nature of the position you are seeking.

III. KINDS OF TESTS

Tests are used for purposes other than measuring knowledge and ability to perform specified duties. For some positions, it is equally important to test ability to make adjustments to new situations or to profit from training. In others, basic mental abilities not dependent on information are essential. Questions which test these things may not appear as pertinent to the duties of the position as those which test for knowledge and information. Yet they are often highly important parts of a fair examination. For very general questions, it is almost impossible to help you direct your study efforts. What we can do is to point out some of the more common of these general abilities needed in public service positions and describe some typical questions.

1) General information

Broad, general information has been found useful for predicting job success in some kinds of work. This is tested in a variety of ways, from vocabulary lists to questions about current events. Basic background in some field of work, such as sociology or economics, may be sampled in a group of questions. Often these are principles which have become familiar to most persons through exposure rather than through formal training. It is difficult to advise you how to study for these questions; being alert to the world around you is our best suggestion.

2) Verbal ability

An example of an ability needed in many positions is verbal or language ability. Verbal ability is, in brief, the ability to use and understand words. Vocabulary and grammar tests are typical measures of this ability. Reading comprehension or paragraph interpretation questions are common in many kinds of civil service tests. You are given a paragraph of written material and asked to find its central meaning.

3) Numerical ability

Number skills can be tested by the familiar arithmetic problem, by checking paired lists of numbers to see which are alike and which are different, or by interpreting charts and graphs. In the latter test, a graph may be printed in the test booklet which you are asked to use as the basis for answering questions.

4) Observation

A popular test for law-enforcement positions is the observation test. A picture is shown to you for several minutes, then taken away. Questions about the picture test your ability to observe both details and larger elements.

5) Following directions

In many positions in the public service, the employee must be able to carry out written instructions dependably and accurately. You may be given a chart with several columns, each column listing a variety of information. The questions require you to carry out directions involving the information given in the chart.

6) Skills and aptitudes

Performance tests effectively measure some manual skills and aptitudes. When the skill is one in which you are trained, such as typing or shorthand, you can practice. These tests are often very much like those given in business school or high school courses. For many of the other skills and aptitudes, however, no short-time preparation can be made. Skills and abilities natural to you or that you have developed throughout your lifetime are being tested.

Many of the general questions just described provide all the data needed to answer the questions and ask you to use your reasoning ability to find the answers. Your best preparation for these tests, as well as for tests of facts and ideas, is to be at your physical and mental best. You, no doubt, have your own methods of getting into an exam-taking mood and keeping "in shape." The next section lists some ideas on this subject.

IV. KINDS OF QUESTIONS

Only rarely is the "essay" question, which you answer in narrative form, used in civil service tests. Civil service tests are usually of the short-answer type. Full instructions for answering these questions will be given to you at the examination. But in case this is your first experience with short-answer questions and separate answer sheets, here is what you need to know:

1) Multiple-choice Questions

Most popular of the short-answer questions is the "multiple choice" or "best answer" question. It can be used, for example, to test for factual knowledge, ability to solve problems or judgment in meeting situations found at work.

A multiple-choice question is normally one of three types—
- It can begin with an incomplete statement followed by several possible endings. You are to find the one ending which *best* completes the statement, although some of the others may not be entirely wrong.
- It can also be a complete statement in the form of a question which is answered by choosing one of the statements listed.

- It can be in the form of a problem – again you select the best answer.

Here is an example of a multiple-choice question with a discussion which should give you some clues as to the method for choosing the right answer:

When an employee has a complaint about his assignment, the action which will *best* help him overcome his difficulty is to
   A. discuss his difficulty with his coworkers
   B. take the problem to the head of the organization
   C. take the problem to the person who gave him the assignment
   D. say nothing to anyone about his complaint

In answering this question, you should study each of the choices to find which is best. Consider choice "A" – Certainly an employee may discuss his complaint with fellow employees, but no change or improvement can result, and the complaint remains unresolved. Choice "B" is a poor choice since the head of the organization probably does not know what assignment you have been given, and taking your problem to him is known as "going over the head" of the supervisor. The supervisor, or person who made the assignment, is the person who can clarify it or correct any injustice. Choice "C" is, therefore, correct. To say nothing, as in choice "D," is unwise. Supervisors have and interest in knowing the problems employees are facing, and the employee is seeking a solution to his problem.

2) True/False Questions

The "true/false" or "right/wrong" form of question is sometimes used. Here a complete statement is given. Your job is to decide whether the statement is right or wrong.

SAMPLE: A roaming cell-phone call to a nearby city costs less than a non-roaming call to a distant city.

This statement is wrong, or false, since roaming calls are more expensive.

This is not a complete list of all possible question forms, although most of the others are variations of these common types. You will always get complete directions for answering questions. Be sure you understand *how* to mark your answers – ask questions until you do.

V. RECORDING YOUR ANSWERS

Computer terminals are used more and more today for many different kinds of exams.

For an examination with very few applicants, you may be told to record your answers in the test booklet itself. Separate answer sheets are much more common. If this separate answer sheet is to be scored by machine – and this is often the case – it is highly important that you mark your answers correctly in order to get credit.

An electronic scoring machine is often used in civil service offices because of the speed with which papers can be scored. Machine-scored answer sheets must be marked with a pencil, which will be given to you. This pencil has a high graphite content which responds to the electronic scoring machine. As a matter of fact, stray dots may register as answers, so do not let your pencil rest on the answer sheet while you are pondering the correct answer. Also, if your pencil lead breaks or is otherwise defective, ask for another.

Since the answer sheet will be dropped in a slot in the scoring machine, be careful not to bend the corners or get the paper crumpled.

The answer sheet normally has five vertical columns of numbers, with 30 numbers to a column. These numbers correspond to the question numbers in your test booklet. After each number, going across the page are four or five pairs of dotted lines. These short dotted lines have small letters or numbers above them. The first two pairs may also have a "T" or "F" above the letters. This indicates that the first two pairs only are to be used if the questions are of the true-false type. If the questions are multiple choice, disregard the "T" and "F" and pay attention only to the small letters or numbers.

Answer your questions in the manner of the sample that follows:

32. The largest city in the United States is
 A. Washington, D.C.
 B. New York City
 C. Chicago
 D. Detroit
 E. San Francisco

1) Choose the answer you think is best. (New York City is the largest, so "B" is correct.)
2) Find the row of dotted lines numbered the same as the question you are answering. (Find row number 32)
3) Find the pair of dotted lines corresponding to the answer. (Find the pair of lines under the mark "B.")
4) Make a solid black mark between the dotted lines.

VI. BEFORE THE TEST

Common sense will help you find procedures to follow to get ready for an examination. Too many of us, however, overlook these sensible measures. Indeed, nervousness and fatigue have been found to be the most serious reasons why applicants fail to do their best on civil service tests. Here is a list of reminders:

- Begin your preparation early – Don't wait until the last minute to go scurrying around for books and materials or to find out what the position is all about.
- Prepare continuously – An hour a night for a week is better than an all-night cram session. This has been definitely established. What is more, a night a week for a month will return better dividends than crowding your study into a shorter period of time.
- Locate the place of the exam – You have been sent a notice telling you when and where to report for the examination. If the location is in a different town or otherwise unfamiliar to you, it would be well to inquire the best route and learn something about the building.
- Relax the night before the test – Allow your mind to rest. Do not study at all that night. Plan some mild recreation or diversion; then go to bed early and get a good night's sleep.
- Get up early enough to make a leisurely trip to the place for the test – This way unforeseen events, traffic snarls, unfamiliar buildings, etc. will not upset you.
- Dress comfortably – A written test is not a fashion show. You will be known by number and not by name, so wear something comfortable.

- Leave excess paraphernalia at home – Shopping bags and odd bundles will get in your way. You need bring only the items mentioned in the official notice you received; usually everything you need is provided. Do not bring reference books to the exam. They will only confuse those last minutes and be taken away from you when in the test room.
- Arrive somewhat ahead of time – If because of transportation schedules you must get there very early, bring a newspaper or magazine to take your mind off yourself while waiting.
- Locate the examination room – When you have found the proper room, you will be directed to the seat or part of the room where you will sit. Sometimes you are given a sheet of instructions to read while you are waiting. Do not fill out any forms until you are told to do so; just read them and be prepared.
- Relax and prepare to listen to the instructions
- If you have any physical problem that may keep you from doing your best, be sure to tell the test administrator. If you are sick or in poor health, you really cannot do your best on the exam. You can come back and take the test some other time.

VII. AT THE TEST

The day of the test is here and you have the test booklet in your hand. The temptation to get going is very strong. Caution! There is more to success than knowing the right answers. You must know how to identify your papers and understand variations in the type of short-answer question used in this particular examination. Follow these suggestions for maximum results from your efforts:

1) Cooperate with the monitor

The test administrator has a duty to create a situation in which you can be as much at ease as possible. He will give instructions, tell you when to begin, check to see that you are marking your answer sheet correctly, and so on. He is not there to guard you, although he will see that your competitors do not take unfair advantage. He wants to help you do your best.

2) Listen to all instructions

Don't jump the gun! Wait until you understand all directions. In most civil service tests you get more time than you need to answer the questions. So don't be in a hurry. Read each word of instructions until you clearly understand the meaning. Study the examples, listen to all announcements and follow directions. Ask questions if you do not understand what to do.

3) Identify your papers

Civil service exams are usually identified by number only. You will be assigned a number; you must not put your name on your test papers. Be sure to copy your number correctly. Since more than one exam may be given, copy your exact examination title.

4) Plan your time

Unless you are told that a test is a "speed" or "rate of work" test, speed itself is usually not important. Time enough to answer all the questions will be provided, but this does not mean that you have all day. An overall time limit has been set. Divide the total time (in minutes) by the number of questions to determine the approximate time you have for each question.

5) Do not linger over difficult questions

If you come across a difficult question, mark it with a paper clip (useful to have along) and come back to it when you have been through the booklet. One caution if you do this – be sure to skip a number on your answer sheet as well. Check often to be sure that you have not lost your place and that you are marking in the row numbered the same as the question you are answering.

6) Read the questions

Be sure you know what the question asks! Many capable people are unsuccessful because they failed to *read* the questions correctly.

7) Answer all questions

Unless you have been instructed that a penalty will be deducted for incorrect answers, it is better to guess than to omit a question.

8) Speed tests

It is often better NOT to guess on speed tests. It has been found that on timed tests people are tempted to spend the last few seconds before time is called in marking answers at random – without even reading them – in the hope of picking up a few extra points. To discourage this practice, the instructions may warn you that your score will be "corrected" for guessing. That is, a penalty will be applied. The incorrect answers will be deducted from the correct ones, or some other penalty formula will be used.

9) Review your answers

If you finish before time is called, go back to the questions you guessed or omitted to give them further thought. Review other answers if you have time.

10) Return your test materials

If you are ready to leave before others have finished or time is called, take ALL your materials to the monitor and leave quietly. Never take any test material with you. The monitor can discover whose papers are not complete, and taking a test booklet may be grounds for disqualification.

VIII. EXAMINATION TECHNIQUES

1) Read the general instructions carefully. These are usually printed on the first page of the exam booklet. As a rule, these instructions refer to the timing of the examination; the fact that you should not start work until the signal and must stop work at a signal, etc. If there are any *special* instructions, such as a choice of questions to be answered, make sure that you note this instruction carefully.

2) When you are ready to start work on the examination, that is as soon as the signal has been given, read the instructions to each question booklet, underline any key words or phrases, such as *least, best, outline, describe* and the like. In this way you will tend to answer as requested rather than discover on reviewing your paper that you *listed without describing*, that you selected the *worst* choice rather than the *best* choice, etc.

3) If the examination is of the objective or multiple-choice type – that is, each question will also give a series of possible answers: A, B, C or D, and you are called upon to select the best answer and write the letter next to that answer on your answer paper – it is advisable to start answering each question in turn. There may be anywhere from 50 to 100 such questions in the three or four hours allotted and you can see how much time would be taken if you read through all the questions before beginning to answer any. Furthermore, if you come across a question or group of questions which you know would be difficult to answer, it would undoubtedly affect your handling of all the other questions.

4) If the examination is of the essay type and contains but a few questions, it is a moot point as to whether you should read all the questions before starting to answer any one. Of course, if you are given a choice – say five out of seven and the like – then it is essential to read all the questions so you can eliminate the two that are most difficult. If, however, you are asked to answer all the questions, there may be danger in trying to answer the easiest one first because you may find that you will spend too much time on it. The best technique is to answer the first question, then proceed to the second, etc.

5) Time your answers. Before the exam begins, write down the time it started, then add the time allowed for the examination and write down the time it must be completed, then divide the time available somewhat as follows:
   - If 3-1/2 hours are allowed, that would be 210 minutes. If you have 80 objective-type questions, that would be an average of 2-1/2 minutes per question. Allow yourself no more than 2 minutes per question, or a total of 160 minutes, which will permit about 50 minutes to review.
   - If for the time allotment of 210 minutes there are 7 essay questions to answer, that would average about 30 minutes a question. Give yourself only 25 minutes per question so that you have about 35 minutes to review.

6) The most important instruction is to *read each question* and make sure you know what is wanted. The second most important instruction is to *time yourself properly* so that you answer every question. The third most important instruction is to *answer every question*. Guess if you have to but include something for each question. Remember that you will receive no credit for a blank and will probably receive some credit if you write something in answer to an essay question. If you guess a letter – say "B" for a multiple-choice question – you may have guessed right. If you leave a blank as an answer to a multiple-choice question, the examiners may respect your feelings but it will not add a point to your score. Some exams may penalize you for wrong answers, so in such cases *only*, you may not want to guess unless you have some basis for your answer.

7) Suggestions
   a. Objective-type questions
      1. Examine the question booklet for proper sequence of pages and questions
      2. Read all instructions carefully
      3. Skip any question which seems too difficult; return to it after all other questions have been answered
      4. Apportion your time properly; do not spend too much time on any single question or group of questions

5. Note and underline key words – *all, most, fewest, least, best, worst, same, opposite*, etc.
6. Pay particular attention to negatives
7. Note unusual option, e.g., unduly long, short, complex, different or similar in content to the body of the question
8. Observe the use of "hedging" words – *probably, may, most likely*, etc.
9. Make sure that your answer is put next to the same number as the question
10. Do not second-guess unless you have good reason to believe the second answer is definitely more correct
11. Cross out original answer if you decide another answer is more accurate; do not erase until you are ready to hand your paper in
12. Answer all questions; guess unless instructed otherwise
13. Leave time for review

  b. Essay questions
1. Read each question carefully
2. Determine exactly what is wanted. Underline key words or phrases.
3. Decide on outline or paragraph answer
4. Include many different points and elements unless asked to develop any one or two points or elements
5. Show impartiality by giving pros and cons unless directed to select one side only
6. Make and write down any assumptions you find necessary to answer the questions
7. Watch your English, grammar, punctuation and choice of words
8. Time your answers; don't crowd material

8) Answering the essay question

Most essay questions can be answered by framing the specific response around several key words or ideas. Here are a few such key words or ideas:

M's: manpower, materials, methods, money, management
P's: purpose, program, policy, plan, procedure, practice, problems, pitfalls, personnel, public relations

  a. Six basic steps in handling problems:
1. Preliminary plan and background development
2. Collect information, data and facts
3. Analyze and interpret information, data and facts
4. Analyze and develop solutions as well as make recommendations
5. Prepare report and sell recommendations
6. Install recommendations and follow up effectiveness

  b. Pitfalls to avoid
1. *Taking things for granted* – A statement of the situation does not necessarily imply that each of the elements is necessarily true; for example, a complaint may be invalid and biased so that all that can be taken for granted is that a complaint has been registered

2. *Considering only one side of a situation* – Wherever possible, indicate several alternatives and then point out the reasons you selected the best one
3. *Failing to indicate follow up* – Whenever your answer indicates action on your part, make certain that you will take proper follow-up action to see how successful your recommendations, procedures or actions turn out to be
4. *Taking too long in answering any single question* – Remember to time your answers properly

IX. AFTER THE TEST

Scoring procedures differ in detail among civil service jurisdictions although the general principles are the same. Whether the papers are hand-scored or graded by machine we have described, they are nearly always graded by number. That is, the person who marks the paper knows only the number – never the name – of the applicant. Not until all the papers have been graded will they be matched with names. If other tests, such as training and experience or oral interview ratings have been given, scores will be combined. Different parts of the examination usually have different weights. For example, the written test might count 60 percent of the final grade, and a rating of training and experience 40 percent. In many jurisdictions, veterans will have a certain number of points added to their grades.

After the final grade has been determined, the names are placed in grade order and an eligible list is established. There are various methods for resolving ties between those who get the same final grade – probably the most common is to place first the name of the person whose application was received first. Job offers are made from the eligible list in the order the names appear on it. You will be notified of your grade and your rank as soon as all these computations have been made. This will be done as rapidly as possible.

People who are found to meet the requirements in the announcement are called "eligibles." Their names are put on a list of eligible candidates. An eligible's chances of getting a job depend on how high he stands on this list and how fast agencies are filling jobs from the list.

When a job is to be filled from a list of eligibles, the agency asks for the names of people on the list of eligibles for that job. When the civil service commission receives this request, it sends to the agency the names of the three people highest on this list. Or, if the job to be filled has specialized requirements, the office sends the agency the names of the top three persons who meet these requirements from the general list.

The appointing officer makes a choice from among the three people whose names were sent to him. If the selected person accepts the appointment, the names of the others are put back on the list to be considered for future openings.

That is the rule in hiring from all kinds of eligible lists, whether they are for typist, carpenter, chemist, or something else. For every vacancy, the appointing officer has his choice of any one of the top three eligibles on the list. This explains why the person whose name is on top of the list sometimes does not get an appointment when some of the persons lower on the list do. If the appointing officer chooses the second or third eligible, the No. 1 eligible does not get a job at once, but stays on the list until he is appointed or the list is terminated.

X. HOW TO PASS THE INTERVIEW TEST

The examination for which you applied requires an oral interview test. You have already taken the written test and you are now being called for the interview test – the final part of the formal examination.

You may think that it is not possible to prepare for an interview test and that there are no procedures to follow during an interview. Our purpose is to point out some things you can do in advance that will help you and some good rules to follow and pitfalls to avoid while you are being interviewed.

What is an interview supposed to test?

The written examination is designed to test the technical knowledge and competence of the candidate; the oral is designed to evaluate intangible qualities, not readily measured otherwise, and to establish a list showing the relative fitness of each candidate – as measured against his competitors – for the position sought. Scoring is not on the basis of "right" and "wrong," but on a sliding scale of values ranging from "not passable" to "outstanding." As a matter of fact, it is possible to achieve a relatively low score without a single "incorrect" answer because of evident weakness in the qualities being measured.

Occasionally, an examination may consist entirely of an oral test – either an individual or a group oral. In such cases, information is sought concerning the technical knowledges and abilities of the candidate, since there has been no written examination for this purpose. More commonly, however, an oral test is used to supplement a written examination.

Who conducts interviews?

The composition of oral boards varies among different jurisdictions. In nearly all, a representative of the personnel department serves as chairman. One of the members of the board may be a representative of the department in which the candidate would work. In some cases, "outside experts" are used, and, frequently, a businessman or some other representative of the general public is asked to serve. Labor and management or other special groups may be represented. The aim is to secure the services of experts in the appropriate field.

However the board is composed, it is a good idea (and not at all improper or unethical) to ascertain in advance of the interview who the members are and what groups they represent. When you are introduced to them, you will have some idea of their backgrounds and interests, and at least you will not stutter and stammer over their names.

What should be done before the interview?

While knowledge about the board members is useful and takes some of the surprise element out of the interview, there is other preparation which is more substantive. It *is* possible to prepare for an oral interview – in several ways:

1) Keep a copy of your application and review it carefully before the interview

This may be the only document before the oral board, and the starting point of the interview. Know what education and experience you have listed there, and the sequence and dates of all of it. Sometimes the board will ask you to review the highlights of your experience for them; you should not have to hem and haw doing it.

2) Study the class specification and the examination announcement

Usually, the oral board has one or both of these to guide them. The qualities, characteristics or knowledges required by the position sought are stated in these documents. They offer valuable clues as to the nature of the oral interview. For example, if the job involves supervisory responsibilities, the announcement will usually indicate that knowledge of modern supervisory methods and the qualifications of the candidate as a supervisor will be tested. If so, you can expect such questions, frequently in the form of a hypothetical situation which you are expected to solve. NEVER go into an oral without knowledge of the duties and responsibilities of the job you seek.

3) Think through each qualification required

Try to visualize the kind of questions you would ask if you were a board member. How well could you answer them? Try especially to appraise your own knowledge and background in each area, *measured against the job sought*, and identify any areas in which you are weak. Be critical and realistic – do not flatter yourself.

4) Do some general reading in areas in which you feel you may be weak

For example, if the job involves supervision and your past experience has NOT, some general reading in supervisory methods and practices, particularly in the field of human relations, might be useful. Do NOT study agency procedures or detailed manuals. The oral board will be testing your understanding and capacity, not your memory.

5) Get a good night's sleep and watch your general health and mental attitude

You will want a clear head at the interview. Take care of a cold or any other minor ailment, and of course, no hangovers.

What should be done on the day of the interview?

Now comes the day of the interview itself. Give yourself plenty of time to get there. Plan to arrive somewhat ahead of the scheduled time, particularly if your appointment is in the fore part of the day. If a previous candidate fails to appear, the board might be ready for you a bit early. By early afternoon an oral board is almost invariably behind schedule if there are many candidates, and you may have to wait. Take along a book or magazine to read, or your application to review, but leave any extraneous material in the waiting room when you go in for your interview. In any event, relax and compose yourself.

The matter of dress is important. The board is forming impressions about you – from your experience, your manners, your attitude, and your appearance. Give your personal appearance careful attention. Dress your best, but not your flashiest. Choose conservative, appropriate clothing, and be sure it is immaculate. This is a business interview, and your appearance should indicate that you regard it as such. Besides, being well groomed and properly dressed will help boost your confidence.

Sooner or later, someone will call your name and escort you into the interview room. *This is it.* From here on you are on your own. It is too late for any more preparation. But remember, you asked for this opportunity to prove your fitness, and you are here because your request was granted.

What happens when you go in?

The usual sequence of events will be as follows: The clerk (who is often the board stenographer) will introduce you to the chairman of the oral board, who will introduce you to the other members of the board. Acknowledge the introductions before you sit down. Do not be surprised if you find a microphone facing you or a stenotypist sitting by. Oral interviews are usually recorded in the event of an appeal or other review.

Usually the chairman of the board will open the interview by reviewing the highlights of your education and work experience from your application – primarily for the benefit of the other members of the board, as well as to get the material into the record. Do not interrupt or comment unless there is an error or significant misinterpretation; if that is the case, do not hesitate. But do not quibble about insignificant matters. Also, he will usually ask you some question about your education, experience or your present job – partly to get you to start talking and to establish the interviewing "rapport." He may start the actual questioning, or turn it over to one of the other members. Frequently, each member undertakes the questioning on a particular area, one in which he is perhaps most competent, so you can expect each member to participate in the examination. Because time is limited, you may also expect some rather abrupt switches in the direction the questioning takes, so do not be upset by it. Normally, a board member will not pursue a single line of questioning unless he discovers a particular strength or weakness.

After each member has participated, the chairman will usually ask whether any member has any further questions, then will ask you if you have anything you wish to add. Unless you are expecting this question, it may floor you. Worse, it may start you off on an extended, extemporaneous speech. The board is not usually seeking more information. The question is principally to offer you a last opportunity to present further qualifications or to indicate that you have nothing to add. So, if you feel that a significant qualification or characteristic has been overlooked, it is proper to point it out in a sentence or so. Do not compliment the board on the thoroughness of their examination – they have been sketchy, and you know it. If you wish, merely say, "No thank you, I have nothing further to add." This is a point where you can "talk yourself out" of a good impression or fail to present an important bit of information. Remember, *you close the interview yourself*.

The chairman will then say, "That is all, Mr. _____, thank you." Do not be startled; the interview is over, and quicker than you think. Thank him, gather your belongings and take your leave. Save your sigh of relief for the other side of the door.

How to put your best foot forward

Throughout this entire process, you may feel that the board individually and collectively is trying to pierce your defenses, seek out your hidden weaknesses and embarrass and confuse you. Actually, this is not true. They are obliged to make an appraisal of your qualifications for the job you are seeking, and they want to see you in your best light. Remember, they must interview all candidates and a non-cooperative candidate may become a failure in spite of their best efforts to bring out his qualifications. Here are 15 suggestions that will help you:

1) Be natural – Keep your attitude confident, not cocky

If you are not confident that you can do the job, do not expect the board to be. Do not apologize for your weaknesses, try to bring out your strong points. The board is interested in a positive, not negative, presentation. Cockiness will antagonize any board member and make him wonder if you are covering up a weakness by a false show of strength.

2) Get comfortable, but don't lounge or sprawl

Sit erectly but not stiffly. A careless posture may lead the board to conclude that you are careless in other things, or at least that you are not impressed by the importance of the occasion. Either conclusion is natural, even if incorrect. Do not fuss with your clothing, a pencil or an ashtray. Your hands may occasionally be useful to emphasize a point; do not let them become a point of distraction.

3) Do not wisecrack or make small talk

This is a serious situation, and your attitude should show that you consider it as such. Further, the time of the board is limited – they do not want to waste it, and neither should you.

4) Do not exaggerate your experience or abilities

In the first place, from information in the application or other interviews and sources, the board may know more about you than you think. Secondly, you probably will not get away with it. An experienced board is rather adept at spotting such a situation, so do not take the chance.

5) If you know a board member, do not make a point of it, yet do not hide it

Certainly you are not fooling him, and probably not the other members of the board. Do not try to take advantage of your acquaintanceship – it will probably do you little good.

6) Do not dominate the interview

Let the board do that. They will give you the clues – do not assume that you have to do all the talking. Realize that the board has a number of questions to ask you, and do not try to take up all the interview time by showing off your extensive knowledge of the answer to the first one.

7) Be attentive

You only have 20 minutes or so, and you should keep your attention at its sharpest throughout. When a member is addressing a problem or question to you, give him your undivided attention. Address your reply principally to him, but do not exclude the other board members.

8) Do not interrupt

A board member may be stating a problem for you to analyze. He will ask you a question when the time comes. Let him state the problem, and wait for the question.

9) Make sure you understand the question

Do not try to answer until you are sure what the question is. If it is not clear, restate it in your own words or ask the board member to clarify it for you. However, do not haggle about minor elements.

10) Reply promptly but not hastily

A common entry on oral board rating sheets is "candidate responded readily," or "candidate hesitated in replies." Respond as promptly and quickly as you can, but do not jump to a hasty, ill-considered answer.

11) Do not be peremptory in your answers

A brief answer is proper – but do not fire your answer back. That is a losing game from your point of view. The board member can probably ask questions much faster than you can answer them.

12) Do not try to create the answer you think the board member wants

He is interested in what kind of mind you have and how it works – not in playing games. Furthermore, he can usually spot this practice and will actually grade you down on it.

13) Do not switch sides in your reply merely to agree with a board member

Frequently, a member will take a contrary position merely to draw you out and to see if you are willing and able to defend your point of view. Do not start a debate, yet do not surrender a good position. If a position is worth taking, it is worth defending.

14) Do not be afraid to admit an error in judgment if you are shown to be wrong

The board knows that you are forced to reply without any opportunity for careful consideration. Your answer may be demonstrably wrong. If so, admit it and get on with the interview.

15) Do not dwell at length on your present job

The opening question may relate to your present assignment. Answer the question but do not go into an extended discussion. You are being examined for a *new* job, not your present one. As a matter of fact, try to phrase ALL your answers in terms of the job for which you are being examined.

Basis of Rating

Probably you will forget most of these "do's" and "don'ts" when you walk into the oral interview room. Even remembering them all will not ensure you a passing grade. Perhaps you did not have the qualifications in the first place. But remembering them will help you to put your best foot forward, without treading on the toes of the board members.

Rumor and popular opinion to the contrary notwithstanding, an oral board wants you to make the best appearance possible. They know you are under pressure – but they also want to see how you respond to it as a guide to what your reaction would be under the pressures of the job you seek. They will be influenced by the degree of poise you display, the personal traits you show and the manner in which you respond.

ABOUT THIS BOOK

This book contains tests divided into Examination Sections. Go through each test, answering every question in the margin. We have also attached a sample answer sheet at the back of the book that can be removed and used. At the end of each test look at the answer key and check your answers. On the ones you got wrong, look at the right answer choice and learn. Do not fill in the answers first. Do not memorize the questions and answers, but understand the answer and principles involved. On your test, the questions will likely be different from the samples. Questions are changed and new ones added. If you understand these past questions you should have success with any changes that arise. Tests may consist of several types of questions. We have additional books on each subject should more study be advisable or necessary for you. Finally, the more you study, the better prepared you will be. This book is intended to be the last thing you study before you walk into the examination room. Prior study of relevant texts is also recommended. NLC publishes some of these in our Fundamental Series. Knowledge and good sense are important factors in passing your exam. Good luck also helps. So now study this Passbook, absorb the material contained within and take that knowledge into the examination. Then do your best to pass that exam.

EXAMINATION SECTION

EXAMINATION SECTION
TEST 1

DIRECTIONS: Each question or incomplete statement is followed by several suggested answers or completions. Select the one that BEST answers the question or completes the statement. *PRINT THE LETTER OF THE CORRECT ANSWER IN THE SPACE AT THE RIGHT.*

1. Stress relieving would MOST likely be used on welds of _____ carbon steel.   1.____

    A. low
    B. medium
    C. high
    D. low and medium

2. The steel used to make a chain would ordinarily be _____ steel.   2.____

    A. low carbon
    B. medium carbon
    C. high carbon
    D. alloy

3. Of the following steels, the MOST readily welded steel is _____ carbon steel.   3.____

    A. low   B. medium   C. high   D. very high

4. The property known as *red hardness* would MOST likely be found in a steel used for making   4.____

    A. nails
    B. structural shapes
    C. rivets
    D. taps and dies

5. Wrought iron is superior to low carbon steel where the PRIMARY consideration is   5.____

    A. high strength
    B. ductility
    C. resistance to corrosion
    D. machineability

6. Of the following metals, the one that is NOT easily spot welded is   6.____

    A. low carbon steel
    B. nickel alloys
    C. stainless steel
    D. aluminum

7. The slag from a coated electrode   7.____

    A. serves no useful purpose
    B. helps produce a more ductile weld
    C. must be removed while the weld is still hot
    D. helps oxides form in the weld

8. When using the oxyacetylene torch to cut steel, the' flame should   8.____

    A. contain an excess of acetylene
    B. contain an excess of oxygen
    C. have just enough oxygen to unite completely with the acetylene
    D. strike the steel at a flat angle

9. The amount of filler metal required for a 3/8-inch fillet weld is equal to the amount required for a J-inch fillet weld multiplied by   9.____

    A. 1 1/2   B. 1 3/4   C. 2   D. 2 1/4

1

10. A steel designated as SAE 1035

    A. contains 0.30% to 0.40% carbon
    B. is an alloy steel
    C. is a low carbon steel
    D. is a high carbon steel

11. Assume that the coupling of an oxygen hose has been smeared with a clean grease.
    This is

    A. *good* because it prevents rust
    B. *bad* because the hose will be hard to handle
    C. *good* because the grease is a preservative for the hose material
    D. *bad* because it could result in an explosion

12. Assume that a welder cracks the valves of the oxygen cylinder and the acetylene cylinder slightly and then closes them before he attached the regulators.
    He does this to

    A. blow away dirt in the valve
    B. identify the gas in the cylinder
    C. make sure that there is pressure in the cylinder
    D. make sure the valve is in operating condition

13. After connecting the regulator to the oxygen cylinder, the next step is to

    A. open the cylinder valve
    B. tighten the regulator pressure-adjusting screw
    C. loosen the regulator pressure-adjusting screw
    D. set the regulator pressure-adjusting screw to the desired working pressure

14. In oxyacetylene cutting, an excessive *drag* or *lag* is

    A. helpful in all cases
    B. more troublesome on straight cuts
    C. more troublesome on curved cuts
    D. helpful on level cuts

15. A respirator would MOST likely be worn when welding

    A. cast iron   B. galvanized iron
    C. low carbon steel   D. aluminum

16. The BEST material for backing bars is

    A. copper   B. steel
    C. cast iron   D. tin

17. Assume that oxyacetylene cutting must be performed in a room with a wood floor.
    The BEST precaution to take is to

    A. sweep the floor thoroughly
    B. wet the floor down with water
    C. place sheet steel on the floor in the vicinity of the cutting
    D. have one man act as a fire watchman

18. The feature which distinguishes resistance welding from other types of welding using electricity is concerned with

    A. voltage   B. current   C. electrode   D. pressure

19. Assume that a fillet weld has an undercut.
    Prevention of undercutting on a similar weld can probably be BEST accomplished by

    A. using a higher welding current
    B. using a smaller electrode diameter
    C. keeping a larger molten weld puddle
    D. increasing the weaving motion of the electrode

20. An objection to shotblasting of a weld before visual examination of the weld for flaws is that shotblasting

    A. removes slag which indicates flaws
    B. does not clean the weld thoroughly
    C. does not remove oxide films
    D. may seal surface cracks

21. The *term boxing* refers to _____ welds.

    A. plug   B. butt   C. spot   D. fillet

22. Incomplete penetration of a groove weld is MOST likely due to

    A. welding speed too slow
    B. gap at base of weld too narrow
    C. electrode diameter too small
    D. welding current too large

23. After a flashback in an oxyacetylene torch, the welder should

    A. relight the torch immediately
    B. shut off the oxygen and acetylene valves of the torch and allow the torch to cool before relighting
    C. shut off the oxygen valve of the torch and relight
    D. increase the oxygen pressure at the regulator to clear out the clogged orifice

24. A spark test is made to identify a metal. With proper pressure exerted, the length of the stream of sparks is about six feet.
    The metal is MOST probably

    A. low carbon steel   B. stainless steel
    C. nickel   D. aluminum

25. The BEST way to prevent the formation of a crater at the end of a weld is to

    A. break the arc with a sharp upward motion as soon as the end of the weld is reached
    B. move the electrode back over the completed weld and break the arc a few inches from the end of the weld
    C. pause at the end of the weld and then slowly withdraw the electrode until the arc breaks
    D. increase the voltage as the electrode nears the end of the weld

Questions 26-30.

DIRECTIONS: Questions 26 through 30 refer to the weld symbols shown below.

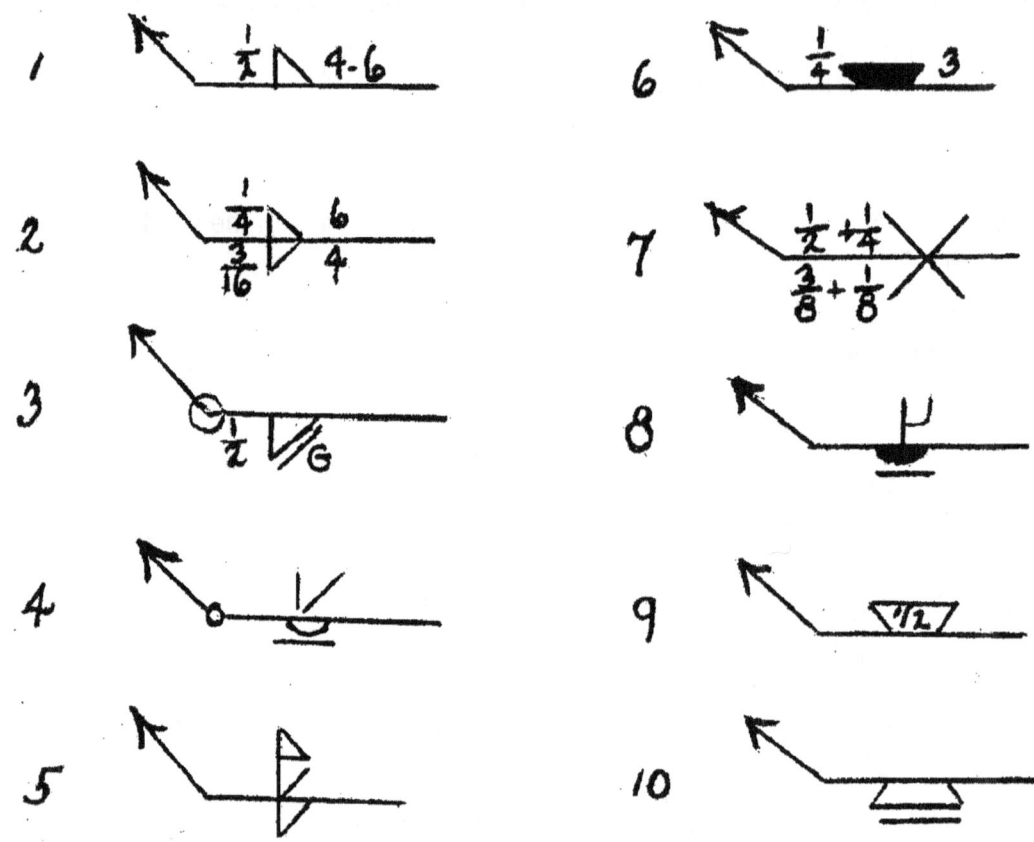

26. The field weld is numbered

    A. 3   B. 4   C. 6   D. 8

27. The weld which extends all around the joint is numbered

    A. 2   B. 3   C. 5   D. 7

28. The intermittent fillet weld is numbered

    A. 1   B. 2   C. 3   D. 5

29. The plug weld which is NOT filled completely is numbered

    A. 6   B. 8   C. 9   D. 10

30. The groove weld which is a melt-thru weld is numbered

    A. 4   B. 5   C. 6   D. 8

31. The cost of arc welding is increased by 31.____

    A. use of smaller diameter electrodes
    B. careful fit-up
    C. use of positioning fixtures
    D. use of setting-up fixtures

32. An electrode stub should be discarded when its length becomes _____ inch(es). 32.____

    A. 4   B. 2   C. 1   D. 1/2

33. It is GOOD welding practice to 33.____

    A. have a powerful fan blow air directly at the welder if he is working in a closed room
    B. weld material which is lying on a concrete floor
    C. ventilate a closed space such as a tank with oxygen "before welding inside the space or tank
    D. leave oxygen and acetylene cylinders outside a tank that is to be welded from the inside

34. When an oxygen cylinder is to be raised by a chain hoist, the hook of the hoist should be attached to 34.____

    A. the valve protection cap
    B. a rope sling around the cylinder
    C. a wire sling around the cylinder
    D. a cradle carrying the cylinder

35. 35.____

    The flame shown above, as seen with welder's goggles, is

    A. oxidizing   B. reducing
    C. neutral   D. stabilizing

36. A back step sequence of welding is MOST often used to 36.____

    A. reduce distortion
    B. increase strength of weld
    C. trap out slag
    D. eliminate undercutting

37. Welding results in the hardening of some metals. This can USUALLY be avoided by 37.____

    A. quenching   B. normalizing
    C. slow cooling   D. carburizing

38. The MAIN reason for the use of flux is to

    A. help the filler metal to adhere to the base metal
    B. remove oxides
    C. prevent overheating of the base metal
    D. replace carbon lost from the base metal during the welding process

39. One of the difficulties encountered in the oxyacetylene welding of aluminum is that aluminum

    A. does not readily form an oxide coating
    B. melts without changing color
    C. welding requires larger torch tips than those required for welding other metals
    D. must be preheated before it can be properly welded

40. The principle advantage of using an oxyhydrogen flame instead of an oxyacetylene flame for the welding of aluminum is that

    A. the lower temperature of the oxyhydrogen flame permits better control of the molten metal
    B. less flux is required with the oxyhydrogen since the flame is not as highly oxidizing as the oxyacetylene
    C. use of the oxyhydrogen flame permits making a weld with less filler rod because of better heat transfer
    D. the oxyhydrogen flame provides better shielding of the molten metal than the oxyacetylene flame

KEY (CORRECT ANSWERS)

1. C	11. D	21. D	31. A
2. A	12. A	22. B	32. B
3. A	13. C	23. B	33. D
4. D	14. C	24. A	34. D
5. C	15. B	25. C	35. B
6. D	16. A	26. B	36. A
7. B	17. C	27. B	37. C
8. B	18. D	28. A	38. B
9. D	19. B	29. C	39. B
10. A	20. D	30. D	40. A

———

TEST 2

DIRECTIONS: Each question or incomplete statement is followed by several suggested answers or completions. Select the one that BEST answers the question or completes the statement. *PRINT THE LETTER OF THE CORRECT ANSWER IN THE SPACE AT THE RIGHT.*

1. At 77°F, the oxygen pressure in a full cylinder of the type used by welders is MOST NEARLY _____ lbs./sq.in.

    A. 700   B. 1200   C. 1700   D. 2200

2. Acetylene cylinders should always be used in an upright position.
   The MAIN reason for not using them when they are lying down is that in this position

    A. it is difficult to control discharge pressure
    B. pressure gages are more easily damaged
    C. cylinders can roll, becoming a safety hazard
    D. acetone will be withdrawn with the acetylene

3. The one of the following methods that is NOT commonly used to correct arc blow is to

    A. reduce the current
    B. increase the arc voltage
    C. weld toward a heavy tack
    D. *back step* on long welds

4. Shrinkage in non-preheated welded products can be reduced to a minimum by

    A. decreasing the size of each pass and increasing the number of passes
    B. avoiding the use of intermittent welds
    C. peening of welds in the cold state, except root and face-layers
    D. increasing the finished thickness of the weld

5. It is MOST important to take precautions to avoid residual stresses when welding

    A. wrought iron   B. mild steel
    C. cast iron   D. low carbon steel

6. When welding steel by the atomic hydrogen welding process, heat for the welding process is produced by the electric arc between

    A. two tungsten electrodes
    B. a steel electrode and the work piece
    C. two carbon electrodes
    D. a tungsten electrode and the work piece

7. Of the following, the MOST important characteristic of the submerged arc welding process is that the

    A. flux is a solid coating on the electrode
    B. arc is not visible while welding
    C. speed of welding is slower than with shielded metal arc welding
    D. process is fully automatic and cannot be used manually

8. Assume that a welding machine is rated for a 60% duty cycle. This means that the

   A. machine can be used only for welding pieces that are 60% of the thickness of a standard piece
   B. generator can be run only 60% of the time during a day
   C. arc can be on for no more than 6 minutes in a 10 minute period
   D. machine cannot supply adequate voltage if more than 60% of the electrode is consumed

9. Rectifier type welding machines are used PRIMARILY to obtain

   A. steady voltage A.C. regardless of length of arc
   B. B.C. current without use of a motor-generator
   C. an initial high voltage A.C. starting arc
   D. adequate D.C. voltage from a low voltage D.C. line

10. With well-designed electrode holders, overheating of the holder will MOST often result from

    A. a poor connection between the cable and the holder
    B. use of excessively long electrodes
    C. welding overhead instead of positioning flat
    D. improper grounding

11. Of the following, the electrode that would be classified as *low hydrogen* is

    A. E-6010   B. E-6012   C. E-6014   D. E-6016

12. The ductility of a metal is its ability to

    A. be welded without preheat
    B. stretch without cracking
    C. absorb alloys during the welding process
    D. retain its strength at all temperatures

13. *Freezing* of the electrode is MOST often caused by

    A. improper grounding of the work
    B. excessive current setting on the welding machine
    C. inability to strike the arc fast enough
    D. wrong electrode for type of work

14. The temperature at which iron melts is MOST NEARLY

    A. 2800°F   B. 4800°F   C. 6800°F   D. 8800°F

15. The oxidizing of aluminum is MOST similar to the

    A. enameling of magnesium   B. annealing of copper
    C. plating of steel   D. rusting of iron

16. Of the following, the metal that is MOST difficult to weld to other metals is

    A. nickel   B. magnesium   C. bronze   D. copper

17. Of the following methods of welding steel, the one for which a flux is NOT generally required is   17.____

    A. vapor shielded   B. submerged arc
    C. electroslag   D. TIG

18. A specific carbon-steel welding electrode is designated by a four digit number. The positions in which this electrode can be used is indicated by the _____ digit.   18.____

    A. 1st   B. 2nd   C. 3rd   D. 4th

19. The E-6013 electrode is MOST suitable for welding   19.____

    A. where deep penetration is required
    B. thin sheet steel
    C. under poor fit-up conditions
    D. when underbead cracking is a problem

20. The PRINCIPAL hardening agent in steel is   20.____

    A. carbon   B. silicon   C. phosphorus   D. sulphur

21. Internal stresses in a hardened steel are BEST relieved by   21.____

    A. normalizing   B. quenching
    C. tempering   D. carburizing

22. *Crater cracks* are caused MAINLY by   22.____

    A. slag inclusions
    B. improper joint preparation
    C. hot shrinkage
    D. improper angle of electrode

23. Slag inclusions are MOST common in welds made in the _____ position.   23.____

    A. flat   B. horizontal
    C. vertical   D. overhead

24. When welding structural steel outdoors in freezing weather, it is poor practice to strike the arc on the base metal at a point outside of the groove MAINLY because   24.____

    A. cracks would tend to start at this point
    B. the resulting weld would be unsightly
    C. it is difficult to hold the arc and transfer it to the groove
    D. weld spatter becomes more of a problem

25. A good rule to follow when welding very high carbon (over 1% carbon) steels is to   25.____

    A. get as much penetration as possible
    B. weld at a fairly high speed
    C. coat the surfacing of the parent metal with a stainless electrode first
    D. make flat beads

26. Of the following, the MOST important cause of underbead cracking is 26.____

    A. hardening of the surface of the parent metal
    B. excessive preheat
    C. too slow cooling of the weld
    D. running stringer beads instead of weaving

27. With respect to groove welding of alloy steel, the one of the following statements that is 27.____
    CORRECT is:
    Cracks in the root bead can

    A. be burnt out by deep penetration on the second pass
    B. be repaired by post heating on the second pass
    C. be corrected by increasing the interpass temperature
    D. not be melted out on the second pass

28. Of the following methods, grooving of cast iron prior to arc welding is BEST done by 28.____

    A. sawing   B. flame cutting
    C. arc cutting   D. grinding

29. Of the following types of cast iron, the one for which welding is NOT generally recom- 29.____
    mended is _____ iron.

    A. white cast   B. gray cast
    C. malleable   D. nodular

30. The one of the following metals that is NOT hardened by cold working is 30.____

    A. copper   B. steel   C. tin   D. aluminum

31. Copper is BEST annealed by 31.____

    A. heating and quenching in water
    B. cold working
    C. precipitation aging
    D. drawing

32. The one of the following that is a common hard surfacing alloy is 32.____

    A. chromium nickel   B. silicon oxide
    C. sintered manganese   D. tungsten carbide

33. Deep penetration should be avoided when arc welding cast iron MAINLY in order to 33.____

    A. reduce carbon pick-up from the parent metal
    B. eliminate the necessity of preheating
    C. speed up cooling of the metal
    D. prevent tempering of the base metal

34. Of the following types of electrodes, the BEST one to use in arc welding malleable iron is 34.____

    A. mild steel   B. nickel base
    C. coated bronze   D. low hydrogen

35. MOST tool steels are characterized by a high _____ content. 35.____

    A. phosphorous B. sulphur
    C. carbon D. nickel

36. Of the following, the one that is the MOST likely cause of weld spatter is 36.____

    A. too low a welding current
    B. too small an electrode
    C. wrong polarity
    D. use of uncoated electrode

37. Porosity in a weld can be reduced by proper welding procedure. 37.____
    The one of the following procedures that will help to produce non-porous welds is to

    A. keep welding currents high
    B. puddle the weld
    C. use a series of stringer beads instead of weaving passes
    D. avoid the use of low hydrogen electrodes

38. The electrode MOST suited to high speed welding in the flat position is the 38.____

    A. E-6010 B. E-6014 C. E-6017 D. E-6020

39. Arc blow refers to the 39.____

    A. force with which the arc hits the base metal
    B. depth of penetration of the arc
    C. jumping of the arc away from the point at which the electrode is directed
    D. voltage that forces the arc across the gap

40. The one of the following that gives the CORRECT order of melting of the metals starting 40.____
    with the one that melts at the LOWEST temperature is

    A. tin, lead, copper, silver
    B. tin, lead, silver, copper
    C. lead, tin, silver, copper
    D. lead, tin, copper, silver

KEY (CORRECT ANSWERS)

1. D	11. D	21. C	31. A
2. D	12. B	22. C	32. D
3. B	13. C	23. D	33. A
4. C	14. A	24. A	34. C
5. C	15. D	25. C	35. C
6. A	16. B	26. A	36. C
7. B	17. D	27. D	37. B
8. C	18. C	28. A	38. D
9. B	19. B	29. A	39. C
10. A	20. A	30. C	40. B

EXAMINATION SECTION
TEST 1

DIRECTIONS: Each question or incomplete statement is followed by several suggested answers or completions. Select the one that BEST answers the question or completes the statement. *PRINT THE LETTEE OF THE CORRECT ANSWER IN THE SPACE AT THE RIGHT.*

1. Of the following, the type of welding in which a filler rod is COMMONLY used is 1.____

   A. resistance   B. carbon arc   C. spot   D. pressure

2. A small short bead used as a temporary fastener is known as a(n) _____ weld. 2.____

   A. spot   B. edge   C. plug   D. tack

3. The one of the following which is the MOST important reason for using the step-back method of welding is to 3.____

   A. increase the strength of the weld
   B. speed the process of welding
   C. reduce the amount of warping
   D. decrease formation of slag

4. In butt welds, the purpose of open roots is to 4.____

   A. reduce the amount of electrode required
   B. secure more overlap
   C. aid slag formation
   D. obtain better penetration

5. Stresses in a welded piece may be relieved by 5.____

   A. annealing   B. case hardening
   C. cold drawing   D. quenching

6. Brazing is MOST commonly done at tempera.tures ranging from *approximately* 6.____

   A. 300° to 900° F   B. 1100° to 2000° F
   C. 2300° to 3000° F   D. 3300° to 3800° F

7. Bronze welding is MOST commonly used for welding 7.____

   A. wrought iron   B. aluminum
   C. white metal   D. chrome steel

Questions 8-11.

DIRECTIONS: In Questions 8 to 11, inclusive, there are shown in Column I various welding symbols. Column II gives types of welds. For each symbol listed in Column I, enter in the appropriate space on the right the capital letter in front *of* the type of weld listed in Column II which the symbol illustrates.

15

COLUMN I	COLUMN II
8. ⌒	A. flush
	B. plug
	C. weld all around
9. │	D. square
	E. bevel
	F. fillet
	G. bead
10. ◿	
11. ○	

12. The one of the following which indicates an intermittent weld is

    A. [symbol]   B. [symbol]   C. [symbol]   D. [symbol]

13. The throat of a 1/2 inch fillet weld is MOST NEARLY _____ inches.

    A. .25   B. .35   C. .45   D. .55

14. Spelter is MOST commonly used in

    A. electric arc welding   B. oxy-acetylene fusion welding
    C. brazing   D. quenching

15. If one dozen 1/8" welding rods cost 48 cents, 37 rods would cost

    A. $1.44   B. $1.48   C. $1.52   D. $1.56

16. The sum of the following numbers, 6 5/8, 3 3/4, 4 1/2, 5 1/8, is

    A. 19 3/4   B. 19 7/8   C. 20   D. 20 1/8

17. Of the following, the one that is a method used to test completed welds is

    A. soaking bath   B. electrolytic resistance
    C. photo-elastic strain   D. acid-etch

18. Of the following, the term that defines a defect in a weld is

    A. scarf   B. tuyere   C. cold shut   D. cohesion

19. When clean steel is heated to a faint straw color, the temperature of the steel, based upon this color, is APPROXIMATELY

    A. 400° F   B. 600° F   C. 800° F   D. 1000° F

20. Of the following metals, the one that has a fibrous structure is

   A. gray cast iron
   B. manganese steel
   C. low carbon steel
   D. wrought iron

21. Of the following alloying elements, the one that is MOST commonly used in tool steel is

   A. manganese   B. zirconium   C. titanium   D. tungsten

22. Of the following automotive parts, the one for which welding of any type would be LEAST desirable is

   A. crankcase
   B. crankshaft
   C. cylinder block
   D. body

23. Of the following metals, the one that is MOST commonly *hard-faced* is

   A. aluminum
   B. bronze
   C. monel
   D. high speed steel

24. Studs are frequently used to strengthen the welds in

   A. iron castings
   B. structural steel
   C. bronze bushings
   D. tool steel

25. Incomplete penetration in a weld is MOST likely to be caused by too

   A. rigid a joint
   B. large a welding rod
   C. large a welding tip
   D. slow a welding speed

26. Of the following, the metal with the LOWEST melting point is

   A. aluminum   B. bronze   C. monel   D. cast iron

27. Quenching to harden steel is MOST commonly done in a bath of

   A. lye   B. soda-ash   C. brine   D. muriatic acid

28. Shrinkage due to welding in non-preheated pieces can be reduced by

   A. open roots
   B. peening
   C. large welds
   D. increased number of welds

29. Brazing is MOST commonly used on

   A. lead   B. bronze   C. babbit   D. aluminum

30. Impact resisting pads on all types of machinery are MOST frequently made of

   A. monel   B. aluminum   C. bronze   D. inconel

31. Drag is usually determined in relation to the consumption of

   A. oxygen   B. acetylene   C. rod   D. power

Questions 32-35.

DIRECTIONS: Questions 32 to 35, inclusive, refer to the paragraph below. These questions are to be answered in strict accordance with the material in this paragraph.

Welds in sheet metal up to 1/16 inch in thickness can be made satisfactorily by flanging the edges of the joint. The edges are prepared by turning up a very thin lip or flange along the line of the joint. The height of this flange should be equal to the thickness of the sheet being welded. The edges should be alined so that the flanges stand up, and the joint should be tack-welded every 5 or 6 inches. Heavy angles or bars should be clamped on each side of the joint to prevent distortion or buckling. No filler metal is required for making this joint. The raised edges are quickly melted by the heat of the welding flame so as to produce an even weld bead which is nearly flush with the original sheet metal surface. By controlling the speed of welding and the motion of the flame, good fusion to the underside of the sheets can be obtained without burning through.

32. According to the above paragraph, satisfactory welds may be made in sheet metal by flanging the edges.
    The MAXIMUM thickness of metal recommended is

    A. 20 gauge   B. 18 gauge   C. 1/16"   D. 5/64"

33. According to the above paragraph, good fusion may be obtained without burning through of the metal by controlling the motion of the flame and the

    A. size of tip   B. speed of welding
    C. oxygen flow   D. acetylene flow

34. According to the above paragraph, if the thickness of the metal is 1/32", then the flange height should be

    A. 1/64"   B. 1/32"   C. 1/16"   D. 1/8"

35. According to the above paragraph, distortion in the welding of sheet metal may be prevented by

    A. controlling the speed of welding
    B. use of a flange of correct height
    C. use of proper filler metal
    D. clamping angles on each side of the joint

KEY (CORRECT ANSWERS)

1. B
2. D
3. C
4. D
5. A

6. B
7. A
8. G
9. D
10. F

11. C
12. D
13. B
14. C
15. B

16. C
17. D
18. C
19. A
20. D

21. D
22. B
23. C
24. A
25. B

26. A
27. C
28. B
29. B
30. C

31. A
32. C
33. B
34. B
35. D

TEST 2

DIRECTIONS: Each question or incomplete statement is followed by several suggested answers or completions. Select the one that BEST answers the question or completes the statement. *PRINT THE LETTER OF THE CORRECT ANSWER IN THE SPACE AT THE RIGHT.*

Questions 1-4.

DIRECTIONS: Questions 1 through 4, inclusive, refer to the jig for testing welded specimens shown below. The jig is to be built up from plate by welding.

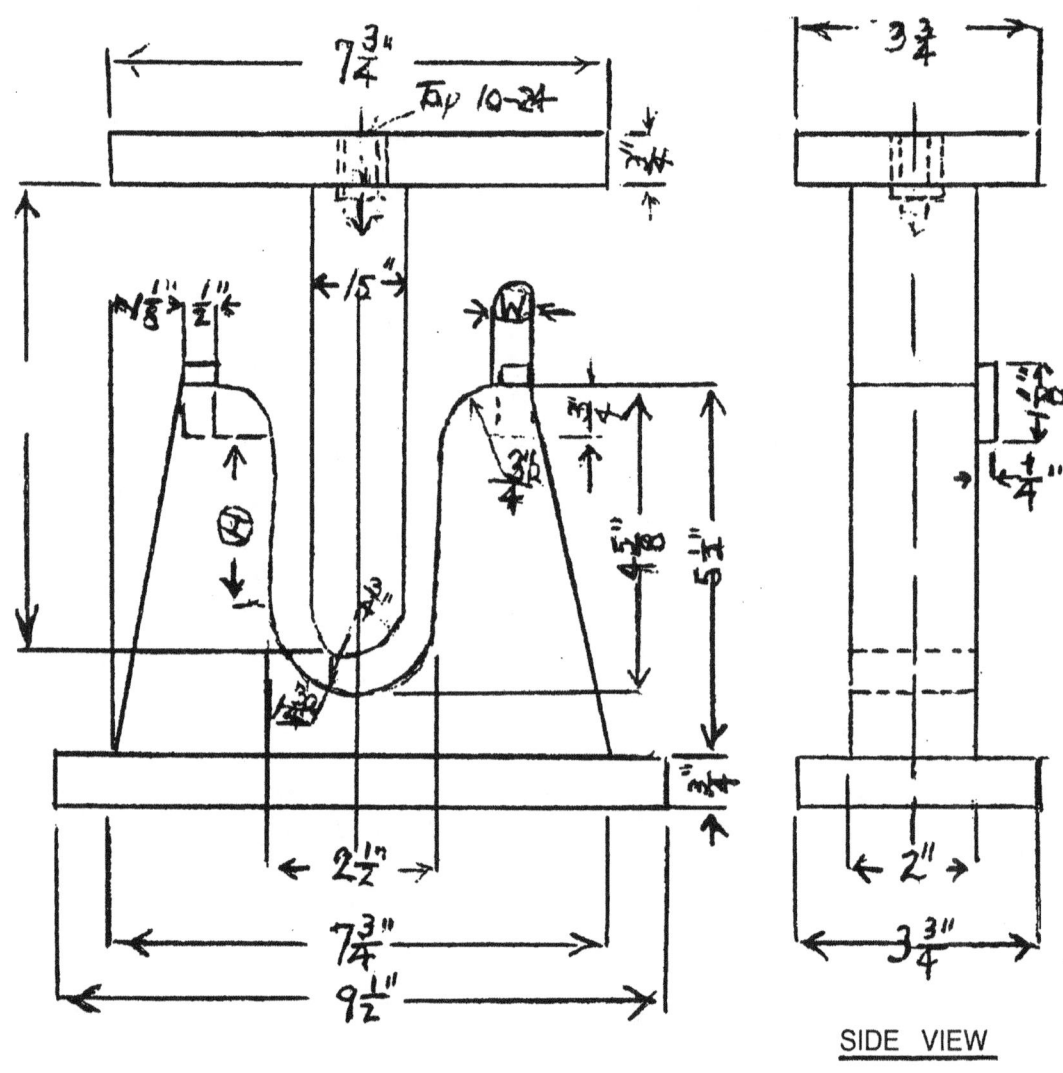

FRONT VIEW   SIDE VIEW

1. The type of weld that would MOST probably be used to weld the plates together is   1.____

   A. V bevel   B. U groove   C. plug   D. fillet

2. The symbol *Tap 10-24* at the top of the jig means that the hole is   2.____

   A. reamed   B. broached   C. threaded   D. punched

3. The length of the straight portion of the jig indicated by the letter *H* is

   A. 2 3/8"   B. 2 1/2"   C. 2 5/8"   D. 2 3/4"

4. The length of the straight portion of the jig indicated by the letter *W* is

   A. 3/4"   B. 7/8"   C. 1"   D. 1 1/8"

Questions 5-21.

DIRECTIONS: Questions 5 through 21, inclusive, are to be answered on the basis of welding with an electric arc welder.

5. Of the following, the MINIMUM voltage necessary to strike an arc with an alternating current machine is, in volts,

   A. 20   B. 40   C. 100   D. 140

6. According to the rules of the Department of Water Supply, Gas and Electricity, the MAXIMUM length of flexible cord or cable permitted for supplying current to a portable welder is _____ feet.

   A. 10   B. 20   C. 30   D. 40

7. The MINIMUM voltage required to strike an arc with a direct current welder is

   A. less than that required for an alternating current welder
   B. more than that required for an alternating current welder
   C. the same as that required for an alternating current welder
   D. more or less than that required for an alternating current welder depending on the type of electrode

8. Of the following, the one that would be MOST likely to appear on the name plate of an arc welder would be

   A. temperature of arc   B. number of feeders
   C. voltage   D. frequency

9. Splattering of the weld is caused by

   A. excessive current   B. too little current
   C. improper flux   D. lack of preheat

10. For a given voltage and current setting on an electric arc welder, decreasing the length of the arc

    A. increases the penetration
    B. decreases the penetration
    C. has no effect on the penetration
    D. may increase or decrease the penetration, depending on the voltage-current setting

11. For a given voltage and current setting on an electric arc welder, when the arc length is shortened, the arc voltage

   A. increases
   B. decreases
   C. stays constant
   D. may increase or decrease, depending on the electrode being used

12. Welding of light gauge metals requires _____ electrodes and _____ voltages.

   A. large; high
   B. large; low
   C. small; high
   D. small; low

13. In straight polarity,

   A. both the electrode and the work are negative
   B. both the electrode and the work are positive
   C. the electrode is negative, the work is positive
   D. the electrode is positive, the work is negative

14. Freezing of the electrode is caused by

   A. insufficient current
   B. electrode being held too long in contact with the work
   C. work not being clean
   D. improper electrode for work being done

15. When welding metal of the same thickness with the same electrode, in the overhead and in the flat position, welding in the overhead position USUALLY requires

   A. less voltage than the flat position
   B. more voltage than the flat position
   C. the same voltage as the flat position
   D. more or less voltage than the flat position depending on the metal being welded

16. Compared with a bare electrode, a shielded electrode produces

   A. more nitrides
   B. more oxidation
   C. a hotter arc
   D. a more stable arc

17. Arc blow is MOST commonly corrected by

   A. welding away from the ground
   B. changing the polarity of the electrode
   C. increasing the voltage
   D. decreasing the current

18. Preheating is MOST commonly used when welding

   A. high manganese-cast steel
   B. chrome-nickel stainless steel
   C. wrought iron
   D. bronze

19. When welding with a shielded electrode, the slag formed 19.____

    A. increases the rate of cooling of weld metal
    B. helps prevent warping
    C. slows the speed of welding
    D. removes oxides from the weld

20. When welding with an electric arc, you find that the arc has a hissing and steady sputtering sound. 20.____
    The MOST probable cause of this is

    A. low voltage   B. low current
    C. high voltage   D. high current

21. When welding in the flat position with 3/8" bare electrodes, the *approximate* range of amperes that would be used is MOST NEARLY 21.____

    A. 40 to 60   B. 110 to 150   C. 250 to 300   D. 450 to 550

Questions 22-35.

DIRECTIONS: Questions 22 through 35, inclusive, are to be answered on the basis of welding with an oxy-acetylene flame.

22. The color of the hose used to connect the torch to the acetylene cylinder is 22.____

    A. green   B. yellow   C. red   D. black

23. The tool MOST commonly used to clean a torch tip is a 23.____

    A. drill   B. file   C. scriber   D. reamer

24. To test for leaks in an oxy-acetylene torch, you should use 24.____

    A. a match   B. #6 fuel oil
    C. soapy water   D. carbon tetrachloride

25. Of the following statements relative to oxygen or acetylene cylinders, the one that is MOST NEARLY CORRECT is: 25.____

    A. Oxygen may be used in place of compressed air in compressed air equipment
    B. A wrench should not be used to open an oxygen cylinder valve
    C. A frozen acetylene cylinder valve should be thawed with boiling water
    D. Oxygen cylinders should be stored lying down

26. Acetylene is USUALLY used at a pressure of less than _____ lbs./sq.in. 26.____

    A. 15   B. 30   C. 45   D. 60

27. The hottest part of a neutral oxy-acetylene flame is located APPROXIMATELY 27.____

    A. at the outermost tip of the flame
    B. midway between the tip of the flame and the tip of the inner cone
    C. at the tip of the inner cone
    D. at the tip of the torch

28. The number of distinct flame zones in a reducing flame is 28.____

   A. 1   B. 2   C. 3   D. 4

29. A reducing flame has 29.____

   A. more oxygen by volume than acetylene
   B. more acetylene by volume than oxygen
   C. the same volume of oxygen and acetylene
   D. no acetylene

30. Fusion welding of cast steel is MOST commonly done with a(n) _____ flame. 30.____

   A. neutral   B. oxidizing   C. reducing   D. carburizing

31. When welding materials of the same thickness, the one of the following that requires the SMALLEST torch tip is 31.____

   A. cast iron   B. steel
   C. wrought iron   D. aluminum

32. As compared to fusion welding, brazing of the same thickness of steel requires 32.____

   A. a smaller torch tip
   B. a larger torch tip
   C. the same size torch tip
   D. a smaller or larger torch tip depending on the carbon content of the steel

33. Of the following statements relative to hard surfacing, the one that is MOST NEARLY CORRECT is: 33.____

   A. Alloys in hard surfacing rods will not oxidize if a neutral flame is used
   B. A smaller torch tip is used for hard surfacing than is used for fusion welding of steel of the same thickness
   C. Hard surfacing rods are least likely to be used when the part must be heat treated after welding
   D. Hard surfacing is usually done with a rod having a low Rockwell C test

34. Of the following metals to be fusion welded, the one for which a flux is USUALLY used is _____ steel. 34.____

   A. low carbon   B. stainless
   C. carbon-molybdenum   D. nickel alloy

35. A metal, when melted with an oxy-acetylene torch, gives off sparks. This metal MOST likely is 35.____

   A. gray cast iron   B. cast steel
   C. aluminum   D. monel

KEY (CORRECT ANSWERS)

1.	D	16.	D
2.	C	17.	A
3.	C	18.	D
4.	A	19.	D
5.	C	20.	A
6.	D	21.	D
7.	A	22.	C
8.	D	23.	A
9.	A	24.	C
10.	D	25.	B
11.	B	26.	A
12.	C	27.	C
13.	C	28.	C
14.	B	29.	B
15.	A	30.	A

31. D
32. A
33. C
34. B
35. B

EXAMINATION SECTION
TEST 1

DIRECTIONS: Each question or incomplete statement is followed by several suggested answers or completions. Select the one that BEST answers the question or completes the statement. *PRINT THE LETTER OF THE CORRECT ANSWER IN THE SPACE AT THE RIGHT.*

Questions 1-10.

DIRECTIONS: In Questions 1 through 10, there are shown in Column I various welding symbols. For each symbol, print in the space at the right the capital letter preceding the type of weld listed in Column II which it illustrates.

COLUMN I | COLUMN II

1. ⌒

2. ◿

3. |

4. V

5. ⋁

6. Y

7. ⊔

8. ⌂

9. ○

10. ─

A. Bead
B. Bevel groove
C. Fillet
D. Flush
E. J groove
F. Plug and slot
G. Square groove
H. U groove
I. V groove
J. Weld all around
K. Field weld
L. Weld both sides

1.____
2.____
3.____
4.____
5.____
6.____
7.____
8.____
9.____
10.____

Questions 11-15.

DIRECTIONS: In Questions 11 through 15, there are shown in Column I preparations of metal for various types of weld joints. For each joint, print in the space at the right the capital letter preceding the name of the joint listed in Column II which it illustrates.

COLUMN I | COLUMN II

11.

A. Butt

B. Corner

12.

C. Edge

D. Lap

E. Tee

13.

14.

15.

11.____

12.____

13.____

14.____

15.____

Questions 16-20.

DIRECTIONS: In Questions 16 through 20, there are shown in Column I various types of welded joints, each illustrating a common fault. For each joint, print in the space at the right the capital letter preceding the welding fault listed in Column II which it best illustrates.

COLUMN I	COLUMN II	
16.	A. Burned through	16.____
17.	B. Crown beads	
	C. Insufficient thickness through throat	17.____
18.	D. Poor penetration at root	18.____
	E. Undercut at toe	
19.	F. Overlap at toe	19.____
	G. No fusion	
20.		20.____

21. The distance through the center of the weld from the root to the face is called the   21.____

   A. reenforcement   B. root
   C. throat   D. toe

22. Heat developed at the welding joint causes metal to   22.____

   A. contract
   B. expand
   C. remain unchanged
   D. expand or contract, depending on the type of metal

23. When a weld is made in a plane which requires the flame to point upward from below, the position of welding is called   23.____

   A. flat   B. horizontal
   C. vertical   D. overhead

24. The one of the following which is a non-ferrous metal is   24.____

   A. cast iron   B. chrome-nickel
   C. copper   D. steel

25. Of the following metals, the one with the LOWEST melting point is   25.____

   A. copper   B. steel   C. tin   D. tungsten

KEY (CORRECT ANSWERS)

1. A
2. C
3. G
4. I
5. B

6. H
7. E
8. F
9. J
10. D

11. A
12. E
13. D
14. C
15. B

16. C
17. D
18. B
19. E
20. A

21. C
22. B
23. D
24. C
25. C

TEST 2

DIRECTIONS: Each question or incomplete statement is followed by several suggested answers or completions. Select the one that BEST answers the question or completes the statement. *PRINT THE LETTER OF THE CORRECT ANSWER IN THE SPACE AT THE RIGHT.*

Questions 1-29.

DIRECTIONS: Questions 1 through 29, inclusive, are to be answered on the basis of welding with the oxyacetylene flame.

1. In the oxyacetylene process of welding, the elements which combine to produce the welding flame are 1.____
   A. acetylene and oxygen
   B. aluminum powder and iron oxide
   C. carbon and hydrogen
   D. oxygen and hydrogen

2. The elements of acetylene gas are 2.____
   A. calcium carbide, hydrogen, and oxygen
   B. carbon and hydrogen
   C. carbon and oxygen
   D. hydrogen and oxygen

3. The HIGHEST pressure at which acetylene should be used is _____ lbs. per sq. inch. 3.____
   A. 10   B. 15   C. 20   D. 25

4. When dissolved in acetone, acetylene can be compressed into cylinders at pressures up to _____ lbs. per sq. inch. 4.____
   A. 15   B. 29.4   C. 250   D. 300

5. Acetylene cylinders should be stored 5.____
   A. in an upright position in a well-ventilated location
   B. lying on their sides on a metal floor
   C. propped against a metal wall
   D. together with oxygen cylinders

6. The number of turns an acetylene cylinder valve should be opened is 6.____
   A. 1   B. 2   C. 3   D. 4

7. The threads on all acetylene hose connections are 7.____
   A. left hand
   B. right hand
   C. either left or right hand, depending on manufacturerdesired
   D. either left or right hand, depending on pressure

8. The color of the hose making connection between the acetylene regulator and the torch is 8._____

   A. green   B. neutral   C. red   D. white

9. To weld MOST steels, the flame that should be used is the 9._____

   A. carburizing   B. neutral
   C. oxidizing   D. reducing

10. The reducing flame can ALWAYS be recognized by the 10._____

    A. distinct hissing sound
    B. purplish inner cone
    C. presence of two distinct flame zones
    D. presence of three distinct flame zones

11. In welding heavy sections, the method of welding that is PRINCIPALLY used is 11._____

    A. backhand   B. forehand
    C. single layer   D. ripple

12. The method of welding in which the flame is pointed back at the molten puddle and the completed weld is called 12._____

    A. backhand   B. forehand
    C. single layer   D. ripple

13. In welding steel plates of 1-1/8" thickness, the number of passes that should be made in a butt joint is 13._____

    A. 1   B. 2   C. 3   D. 4

14. To weld low carbon steel plate of 1" thickness, the one of the following rod diameters that should be used is 14._____

    A. 1/16"   B. 1/8"   C. 3/16"   D. 1/4"

15. The low pressure welding torch is designed to operate with 15._____

    A. low pressure acetylene and high pressure oxygen
    B. low pressure oxygen and high pressure acetylene
    C. equal pressures of oxygen and acetylene
    D. pressures of oxygen and acetylene dependent on type of work being welded

16. You are using a medium pressure torch with both acetylene and oxygen pressures of 1 lb. per sq. inch.
    The tip size you should use is 16._____

    A. 00   B. 2   C. 4   D. 6

17. Popping out of the flame and the emission of sparks from the tip of the welding torch indicate a 17._____

    A. clogged tip
    B. leaking valve
    C. leak in the mixing head set
    D. out of round tip orifice

18. To increase the depth of fusion in making narrow bead welds in the flat position, _____ the tip angle and _____.

    A. *decrease* both; the welding speed
    B. *decrease;* increase the welding speed
    C. *increase;* the welding speed
    D. *increase;* decrease the welding speed

18.____

19. To weld gray cast iron, the

    A. flame should be pointed in the direction of welding
    B. flame should be pointed towards the finishing weld
    C. rod should be held above the weld and melted drop by drop into the puddle
    D. weld should be done as slowly and carefully as possible

19.____

20. To weld medium carbon steel,

    A. no preheating is advisable
    B. the flame should be adjusted to give an oxidizing mixture
    C. the parts should be cooled as rapidly as possible after welding
    D. the puddle of metal should be kept as small as practicable

20.____

21. To weld high carbon steel,

    A. a low carbon welding rod should be used
    B. no preheating is advisable
    C. the flame should be adjusted to carburizing
    D. the welding should be done as slowly as possible

21.____

22. In cutting with the oxyacetylene flame, the

    A. metal is first preheated with a mixture of acetylene and oxygen
    B. torch is usually held at an angle of 45 to the work
    C. preheating flame is turned off as soon as cutting spot has been raised to bright red heat
    D. preheating flame passes through center hole

22.____

23. To weld stainless steel,

    A. an oxidizing flame is preferable
    B. the metal should be protected from the air during welding
    C. a carburizing flame is preferable
    D. the hot metal should be stirred or puddled with the rod

23.____

24. To weld copper,

    A. a flux must be used
    B. a carburizing flame should be used
    C. the heat required is approximately twice that used for steel of a similar thickness
    D. the end of the steel filler rod should be kept out of the molten puddle

24.____

25. To weld aluminum, 25.____

    A. a highly carburizing flame is advisable
    B. the forehand method should be used
    C. a welding tip one size smaller than that required for steel of the same thickness should be used
    D. the film of aluminum oxide will melt at welding temperature and requires no flux for removal

26. To weld monel metal, 26.____

    A. an oxidizing flame is advisable
    B. a welding tip one size larger than that required for steel of the same thickness should be used
    C. no flux is used
    D. the molten pool of metal should be puddled and boiled

27. In fusion welding of brass, 27.____

    A. only the base metal is melted
    B. only the welding rod is melted
    C. the welding rod and base metal are melted
    D. a flux is not required

28. In bronze welding, 28.____

    A. a flux is not required
    B. dissimilar metals cannot be joined
    C. the base metals joined are not heated to their melting temperature
    D. the metals joined have a lower melting point than the bronze filler rod

29. In brazing, the filter metal 29.____

    A. is a ferrous metal or alloy
    B. is heated only to a red heat
    C. has a melting point lower than $1000°$ F
    D. has a melting point lower than that of the metals or alloys to be joined

30. Of the following metals, the one with the HIGHEST melting point is 30.____

    A. aluminum   B. copper   C. lead   D. steel

KEY (CORRECT ANSWERS)

1. A
2. B
3. B
4. C
5. A

6. A
7. A
8. C
9. B
10. D

11. A
12. A
13. D
14. D
15. A

16. A
17. C
18. D
19. B
20. D

21. C
22. A
23. B
24. C
25. B

26. B
27. C
28. C
29. D
30. D

TEST 3

DIRECTIONS: Each question or incomplete statement is followed by several suggested answers or completions. Select the one that BEST answers the question or completes the statement. *PRINT THE LETTER OF THE CORRECT ANSWER IN THE SPACE AT THE RIGHT.*

Questions 1-20.

DIRECTIONS: Questions 1 through 20, inclusive, are to be answered on the basis of electric arc welding.

1. In welding cast iron with a coated 1/8" electrode having a steel base, the welding current should be kept at APPROXIMATELY _____ amperes.

    A. 80 B. 160 C. 220 D. 240

2. Under average conditions, welding machines should be given a cleaning with clean, dry, compressed air AT LEAST once each

    A. day B. week C. month D. year

3. The voltage across the arc of a D.C. generator driving a D.C. welding machine will usually range from

    A. 1 to 10 B. 15 to 45 C. 20 to 800 D. 60 to 200

4. A.C. welding machines require the use of

    A. four position switches
    B. heavily coated electrodes
    C. low frequency generators
    D. open core transformers

5. In using arc welding machines,

    A. a motor generator type of machine should not be operated with a power ground
    B. circuits should be checked while alive
    C. the polarity switch should be operated while the machine is idling
    D. the rotary switch for current settings should be operated while the machine is operating under the load of a welding current

6. In metal arc welding, the arc is maintained between

    A. two carbon electrodes
    B. two graphite electrodes
    C. two tungsten electrodes
    D. a metal electrode and the base metal

7. The standard length of carbon electrodes is _____ inches.

    A. 6 B. 12 C. 20 D. 24

8. The coating on heavily coated or shielded arc electrodes

    A. increases attractive force between molten metal and the end of the electrode
    B. prevents contamination of metal in arc by oxygen from air
    C. provides ingredients which, when melted, prevent formation of slag over molten metal
    D. reduces arc stability

9. In general, the MAXIMUM size diameter of the lightly coated electrode permissible for vertical and overhead welding positions is

   A. 3/16"   B. 3/8"   C. 1/4"   D. 5/16"

   9.____

10. If the arc keeps going out, it is MOST probably due to the

    A. arc being too short
    B. arc being too long
    C. current setting being too low
    D. speed of electrode travel being too slow

    10.____

11. The heated area on the weld will be increased by a

    A. heavier section of the weld
    B. longer arc length with same setting of welding machine
    C. decreased current at constant speed
    D. decreased speed of welding at constant current

    11.____

12. In straight polarity with a D.C. machine, the electrode is

    A. always negative
    B. always positive
    C. alternately negative and positive
    D. either negative or positive

    12.____

13. In welding medium carbon steel, no preheating is necessary if the electrodes used are

    A. heavily fluxed   B. low carbon
    C. made of bronze   D. made of stainless steel

    13.____

14. In welding high carbon steel, good fusion to the side-walls and root of the joint without excessive penetration can be accomplished by

    A. rapid cooling after welding
    B. excessive puddling
    C. keeping welding heat high
    D. depositing metal in small string beads

    14.____

15. The welding current required for welding copper in relation to that required for steel of the same thickness is ordinarily

    A. lower
    B. higher
    C. the same
    D. dependent on type of arc welding being done

    15.____

16. In arc cutting, a welder should use _____ polarity and a(n) _____ arc.

    A. reversed; short   B. reversed; even
    C. straight; even   D. straight; short

    16.____

17. In bead welding, the electrode should

    A. vary the arc length
    B. be fed down to the work at about half the rate of speed at which the metal is deposited
    C. be moved from side to side
    D. be slightly tilted in the direction of travel

    17._____

18. The condition known as magnetic blow may be BEST corrected by

    A. holding a longer arc
    B. placing the ground in the direction the arc blows from the point of welding
    C. removing the ground
    D. using D.C. current

    18._____

19. An undercut may be MOST probably caused by

    A. insufficient weaving
    B. low speed of welding
    C. puddle of molten metal becoming too small
    D. use of excessive welding current

    19._____

20. A brittle weld may be MOST probably produced by

    A. a bare electrode
    B. a shielded arc electrode
    C. too large an electrode
    D. excessive weaving

    20._____

21. Warping due to excessive local heating at the joint may be BEST prevented by

    A. using electrode with low welding speed
    B. using electrode with high penetrating properties
    C. removing back-up strip
    D. welding rapidly

    21._____

22. The need for preheating of steel will be increased by a

    A. larger welding rod diameter
    B. low atmospheric temperature
    C. low carbon content
    D. low welding speed

    22._____

23. The one of the following metals which will require the LOWEST degree of preheating is

    A. cast iron
    B. copper
    C. low carbon steel (.20% carbon)
    D. tool steel

    23._____

24.

In the joints shown above (plates and angles of V groove being equal), the amount of filler rod required by joint B as compared to A is

A. less
B. more
C. equal
D. dependent on the type of weld to be made

25.

In the joints shown above (with dimensions and plates being equal), the amount of welding rod required by joint A as compared to joint B is

A. less
B. more
C. equal
D. dependent on type of weld to be made

KEY (CORRECT ANSWERS)

1. A
2. C
3. B
4. B
5. C

6. D
7. B
8. B
9. A
10. A

11. D
12. A
13. D
14. D
15. B

16. A
17. D
18. B
19. D
20. A

21. D
22. B
23. C
24. A
25. B

EXAMINATION SECTION
TEST 1

DIRECTIONS: Each question or incomplete statement is followed by several suggested answers or completions. Select the one that BEST answers the question or completes the statement. *PRINT THE LETTER OF THE CORRECT ANSWER IN THE SPACE AT THE RIGHT.*

1. A *flat weld* is made by the fusion welding process in a

    A. horizontal plane
    B. plane inclined at 50° to the horizontal
    C. plane inclined at 20° to the vertical
    D. vertical plane

    1._____

2. The symbol ◣ means

    A. a bead
    B. a triangular groove
    C. weld far side
    D. fillett weld

    2._____

3. The symbol ⌒ means

    A. field weld
    B. plug and slot
    C. bevel weld
    D. flush weld

    3._____

4. The symbol shown at the right means
    A. a flush joint is to be made with square ends
    B. the joint is to be made with members A and B grooved
    C. the joint is to be made with member A grooved
    D. the joint is to be made with member B grooved

    4._____

5. The standard size of a covered filler metal refers to the

    A. diameter of the core wire
    B. diameter of the covered filler metal
    C. circumference of the core wire
    D. circumference of the covered filler metal

    5._____

6. No welding is to be done when the prevailing atmospheric temperature is

    A. 40° F   B. 20° F   C. 25° F   D. 50° F

    6._____

7. In welding 3/4" plates in the vertical position with 3/16" coated electrodes, it is recommended that the current range should be APPROXIMATELY _____ amperes.

    A. 100-150   B. 150-200   C. 200-300   D. 300-350

    7._____

8. In welding 1/2" plates in the flat position with 5/32" coated electrodes, it is recommended that the current range should be APPROXIMATELY _____ amperes.

    A. 90-180   B. 180-250   C. 250-320   D. 320-360

    8._____

41

9. The *throat* dimension of a 3/8" fillet weld is

   A. 0.2645" B. 0.3750" C. 0.2850" D. 0.3000"

10. Fusion welding consists essentially of a localized progressive melting and flowing together of adjacent edges of *base metal* parts by means of a sustained electric arc between a metal electrode and the base metal maintaining a temperatore of APPROXIMATELY

    A. 6000° F B. 10,000° F C. 20,000° F D. 25,000° F

11. Which one of the following statements is CORRECT?

    A. Arc welding processes wherein molten filler, weld and base metals are effectively protected are classified as *unshielded*.
    B. When molten metal is not protected from atmospheric contamination, it absorbs a very small volume of nitrogen.
    C. In direct current bare electrode welding of mild steel, the heat developed at the negative terminal is greater than that developed at the positive terminal.
    D. Covered electrodes are obtainable for either alternating or direct current or for both.

12. Which one of the following statements is CORRECT?

    A. Good short arc of proper voltage is usually indicated by steady snappy crackling sound and steady shower of small sparks.
    B. Too long an arc will hiss and sputter.
    C. Slag should not be cleaned off before the next bead is deposited.
    D. A wide bead should be welded by weaving.

13. When welding a butt joint in 18-gauge sheet metal, the amperage range generally recommended is

    A. 20-30 B. 80-100 C. 35-50 D. 60-80

14. The Lincoln Electric Company's electrode for arc welding of bronze, brass, or copper is called

    A. nickelchromeweld   B. aerisweld
    C. soft weld   D. anode

15. When welding with coated rods, the polarity to be used depends on the

    A. position of the work
    B. amperage used
    C. voltage used
    D. rod manufacturer's recommendation

16. Weld craters are usually caused by

    A. the pressures of the expanding gases and of the electron stream from the electrode tip, both of which blow the liquid metal toward the edges of the crater
    B. the low temperature at the center of the crater
    C. change in the direction of the welding current at the arc terminal
    D. eddy currents

17. The protective equipment usually used by arc welders working with a current of 60 amperes consists of 17.____

    A. head shield and wire brush
    B. face shield and electrode holder
    C. head shield and protective clothing
    D. goggles and gloves

18. The angularity of the electrode to the work 18.____

    A. may determine to a marked degree the quality of the weld metal
    B. has no effect upon the weld metal
    C. does not control the amount of undercutting
    D. does not affect the ease with which filler metal is placed in the weld

19. Shrinkage due to welding can be controlled and reduced to a minimum in non-preheated products by the use of 19.____

    A. closed roots
    B. the minimum use of intermittent welds
    C. the maximum number of welds
    D. low temperature arcs

20. Before welding, heavy sections are usually 20.____

    A. dipped in an oil bath
    B. placed in a room to acquire room temperature
    C. dipped in cold water
    D. preheated

21. Warping due to welding can be controlled and reduced to a minimum in non-preheated products by 21.____

    A. initial distortion   B. using coated electrodes
    C. welding in the open   D. using bare electrodes

22. Which one of the following statements is CORRECT? 22.____

    A. Shielded electrodes have a tendency to freeze the base metal.
    B. Greater speed is obtained with bare arc electrodes than with shielded electrodes.
    C. The composition of the coating determines the best polarity of the electrode.
    D. A useful characteristic of the electrode's coating is its high electrical conductivity.

23. The slag produced when welding with a coated electrode 23.____

    A. speeds up the freezing rate of molten metal
    B. acts as a scavenger in removing oxides and impurities
    C. speeds up the cooling rate of solidified weld metal
    D. distorts the shape of the deposit

24. The symbol means _____ joint welded _____ _____ side(s).   24._____

    A. open square-butt; one   B. open square-butt; both
    C. single-V butt; one   D. single-V butt; both

25. When using a 3/8" diameter graphite electrode for arc cutting, it is recommended to use a current range of _____ amperes.   25._____

    A. 600-800   B. 400-700   C. 200-400   D. 50-200

KEY (CORRECT ANSWERS)

1.	A	11.	D
2.	D	12.	A
3.	B	13.	C
4.	C	14.	B
5.	A	15.	D
6.	B	16.	A
7.	B	17.	C
8.	A	18.	A
9.	A	19.	A
10.	A	20.	D

21. A
22. C
23. B
24. D
25. C

TEST 2

DIRECTIONS: Each question or incomplete statement is followed by several suggested answers or completions. Select the one that BEST answers the question or completes the statement. *PRINT THE LETTER OF THE CORRECT ANSWER IN THE SPACE AT THE RIGHT.*

1. Select the CORRECT statement: 1.____

    A. The arc-cutting process is used extensively for cutting rivets
    B. Coated electrodes cannot be used in arc cutting
    C. Arc cutting cannot be used to pierce holes in plates
    D. The electric arc has proven unsatisfactory for many deseaming operations

2. The term *undercutting* in arc welding means: 2.____

    A. Elongated or globular inclusions in the weld
    B. Failure to dissolve by means of proper fluxing, the oxide or other foreign material present on the surfaces to which the deposited metal must fuse
    C. The reduction in base metal thickness at the line where the last bead is fused to the surface
    D. Gases formed by chemical reactions in the weld

3. In inspecting welds to detect cracks, the oil usually used is _____ oil. 3.____

    A. No. 6   B. cylinder   C. kerosene   D. compound

4. If the current seems too hot but the penetration is poor, the trouble may be due to 4.____

    A. use of the wrong electrode
    B. too high a voltage
    C. dust on the welding surface
    D. water on the welding surface

5. The MOST frequent cause of sparking on a commutator is 5.____

    A. excessive speed of the rotor
    B. too low a voltage
    C. an improperly fitted brush
    D. too high a current

6. If the current of an electric welding machine varies constantly while welding, the trouble usually is 6.____

    A. reversed polarity
    B. poor ground connection
    C. field adjustment out of balance
    D. fuse blown

7. If the electric arc is hard to start and hard to hold, the trouble is usually due to a(n) 7.____

    A. broken lead
    B. heavy intermittent load
    C. dirty generator commutator
    D. improper setting of the rheostats

8. Successful arc welding cannot be accomplished at a voltage lower than _____ volts.

   A. 34   B. 22   C. 18   D. 14

9. The voltage required to strike a D.C. arc is APPROXIMATELY _____ volts.

   A. 75   B. 60   C. 50   D. 40

10. The voltage required to strike an A.C. arc is APPROXIMATELY _____ volts.

    A. 110   B. 85   C. 70   D. 60

11. When the arc stream tends to waiver from its intended path, the action is known as

    A. resistance welding
    B. shielded arc welding
    C. arc blow
    D. weaving

12. The LEAST preferable position in which to do arc welding is

    A. flat
    B. horizontal
    C. vertical
    D. overhead

13. The speed in inches per minute that should be used for arc welding a butt joint with 50% penetration in the flat position, in a 1/2" plate, is APPROXIMATELY

    A. 15   B. 10   C. 5   D. 2

14. The number of beads that should be used when arc welding a butt joint with 100% penetration, in the flat position, using a 5/16" electrode on a 3/8" plate, is

    A. 2   B. 1   C. 4   D. 3

15. The number of beads that should be used when arc welding a 60° scarfed butt joint with 100% penetration, in the flat position, using 5/32" electrode on a 1/2" plate, is

    A. 4   B. 9   C. 6   D. 8

16. In welding cast iron with the hand carbon arc, the dianeter of the point should be APPROXIMATELY _____ the dianeter of the carbon used.

    A. one-quarter
    B. one-half
    C. equal to
    D. three-quarters

17. The MAXIMUM current that should be used with a hand carbon arc using a 1/2" carbon electrode is _____ amperes.

    A. 450   B. 600   C. 700   D. 850

18. In electric fusion welding of mild steel with heavily coated shielded electrodes, if the arc hisses and has a strong sputter, the cause is MOST likely due to

    A. low voltage
    B. low current
    C. rate of feed of electrode too large
    D. high current

19. In arc welding of mild rolled steel in the flat position with bare or washed electrodes, if the arc makes a whistling or hissing and crackling sound, the cause is MOST likely due to

    A. low voltage across arc
    B. high current
    C. high voltage across arc
    D. low current

20. The process of reheating after welding and slowly cooling is called

    A. quenching
    B. case hardening
    C. annealing
    D. oxidizing

21. The angle between bevels in butt welds should be APPROXIMATELY

    A. 90°
    B. 80°
    C. 60°
    D. 30°

22. A weld used to hold parts together for assembly purposes is called a _____ weld.

    A. fillet
    B. tack
    C. butt
    D. lap

23. An arc welder working in the city must be licensed in order to weld

    A. automobile fenders
    B. fire escapes
    C. streetcar tracks
    D. truck bodies

24. Rules for fusion welding are made by the

    A. department of housing and buildings
    B. fire department
    C. board of standards and appeals
    D. civil service commission

25. The starting of any structural welding work is forbidden until an application for a permit to perform such work is filed with and approved by the

    A. chief borough engineer
    B. borough superintendent
    C. chief clerk of the borough
    D. commissioner of borough works

KEY (CORRECT ANSWERS)

1.	A	11.	C
2.	C	12.	D
3.	C	13.	B
4.	A	14.	A
5.	C	15.	D
6.	B	16.	B
7.	D	17.	C
8.	D	18.	A
9.	C	19.	C
10.	B	20.	C

21. C
22. B
23. B
24. C
25. B

———

EXAMINATION SECTION
TEST 1

DIRECTIONS: Each question or incomplete statement is followed by several suggested answers or completions. Select the one that BEST answers the question or completes the statement. *PRINT THE LETTER OF THE CORRECT ANSWER IN THE SPACE AT THE RIGHT.*

1. The MOST commonly used fuel gas is 1.____
   A. butane B. propane C. acetylene D. methane

2. Oxygen is used in conjunction with a fuel gas in order to 2.____
   A. reduce the temperatures generated
   B. support combustion
   C. make fuel gases safer to use
   D. decrease polluting effects

3. _____ creates the GREATEST amount of heat when burned. 3.____
   A. Propane B. Methane C. Butane D. Acetylene

4. An oxyacetylene system uses _____ cylinder(s). 4.____
   A. two B. three C. four D. one

5. Oxygen cylinders are made of 5.____
   A. aluminum B. steel
   C. iron D. all of the above

6. The percentage of oxygen in a cylinder is _____%. 6.____
   A. 50 B. 75 C. 90 D. 100

7. The pressures in oxygen cylinders can range up to ____ psi. 7.____
   A. 1500 B. 2000 C. 2200 D. 2500

8. Oxygen cylinders are ALWAYS painted 8.____
   A. green B. blue C. yellow D. black

9. Acetylene cylinders are ALWAYS painted 9.____
   A. green B. blue C. yellow D. black

10. Inside an acetylene cylinder, there is 10.____
    A. acetylene B. acetone
    C. honeycomb material D. all of the above

11. It is extremely dangerous to use acetylene at pressures above _____ psi. 11.____
    A. 15 B. 25 C. 100 D. 250

49

12. Pure acetylene is _____ when compressed. 12._____

    A. safe B. explosive C. a solid D. cold

13. Both acetylene and oxygen cylinders have 13._____

    A. control valves B. regulators
    C. safety features D. all of the above

14. Acetylene cylinders contain both regulators and _____ as safety devices. 14._____

    A. limiters B. fusible plugs
    C. valves D. caps

15. Portable systems are USUALLY secured to a 15._____

    A. shoulder harness B. hydraulic cart
    C. handtruck D. backpack

16. Both oxygen and acetylene cylinders should ALWAYS be kept in a(n) _____ position. 16._____

    A. upright B. horizontal
    C. inverted D. suspended

17. A manifold oxyacetylene system is often used when work is 17._____

    A. done in several different locations
    B. always done in the workshop
    C. always done at the same stations in the workshop
    D. primarily heating and brazing

18. Oxygen and acetylene are mixed inside the 18._____

    A. hoses B. regulator
    C. torch D. all of the above

19. Regulators control 19._____

    A. internal cylinder pressure
    B. discharge pressure
    C. mixing volume
    D. all of the above

20. Regulators are _____ adjusted. 20._____

    A. automatically B. pneumatically
    C. manually D. hydraulically

21. _____ are used to protect the cylinder valves when not in use. 21._____

    A. Caps B. Cradles C. Cushions D. Covers

22. A special key is needed to 22._____

    A. open the acetylene cylinder
    B. attach the hoses
    C. adjust the flame
    D. adjust the gas mixture

23. The oxyacetylene mixture is _____ ignited.   23._____

    A. automatically   B. manually
    C. spontaneously   D. none of the above

24. The GREATEST fire hazard occurring during the use of oxyacetylene equipment is from   24._____

    A. the extremely hot flame
    B. a cylinder explosion
    C. sparks and hot metals
    D. unexpected heating of combustibles

25. Sparks and hot metal cause APPROXIMATELY _____% of all fires during torch operations.   25._____

    A. 25   B. 50   C. 60   D. 75

KEY (CORRECT ANSWERS)

1. C		11. A	
2. B		12. B	
3. D		13. D	
4. A		14. B	
5. B		15. C	
6. D		16. A	
7. C		17. C	
8. A		18. C	
9. D		19. B	
10. D		20. C	

            21. A
            22. A
            23. B
            24. C
            25. C

TEST 2

DIRECTIONS: Each question or incomplete statement is followed by several suggested answers or completions. Select the one that BEST answers the question or completes the statement. *PRINT THE LETTER OF THE CORRECT ANSWER IN THE SPACE AT THE RIGHT.*

1. All torch operators and fireguards must hold a(n)

    A. operator's license
    B. certificate of fitness
    C. CPR and first aid certificate
    D. all of the above

    1.____

2. The above document must be _____ during all torch operations.

    A. in the operator's possession
    B. on file with the state
    C. on file with the county
    D. on file with the operator's employer

    2.____

3. _____ fireguard(s) is(are) required for each torch operator.

    A. One   B. Two   C. Three   D. Four

    3.____

4. An additional fireguard is required

    A. to circulate between welding stations
    B. on the floor below the work area
    C. on the floor above the work area
    D. all of the above

    4.____

5. The supervisor must

    A. be notified in writing 48 hours before work is done
    B. designate a safe work area
    C. provide a copy of the building safety regulations
    D. all of the above

    5.____

6. The supervisor may NOT be

    A. the cutting or welding contractor
    B. an employee of the building owner
    C. allowed into the cutting or welding station
    D. all of the above

    6.____

7. All of the following are of concern to the supervisor EXCEPT

    A. open duct work or vents
    B. combustible materials
    C. partially filled acetylene cylinders
    D. none of the above

    7.____

8. Oxyacetylene equipment should be approved by

    A. OSHA
    B. the Board of Standards and Appeals
    C. the supervisor
    D. all of the above

9. Safety clothing includes all of the following EXCEPT

    A. protective goggles
    B. fire-resistant gauntlet gloves
    C. an open collar shirt with protective pockets
    D. none of the above

10. All of the following present fire hazards during welding operations EXCEPT

    A. flammable gases   B. paper
    C. asbestos insulation   D. plywood boards

11. The work area should be checked _____ after all torch work is completed.

    A. once   B. twice
    C. three times   D. every hour for six hours

12. A signed inspection report must be completed by

    A. each fireguard
    B. the supervisor
    C. a fire department inspector
    D. the torch operator

13. In order to prevent sprinkler heads from opening during routine torch work, they should be

    A. turned off at the standpipe head
    B. sprayed with water
    C. covered with wet rags
    D. all of the above

14. No flammable materials should be within _____ feet of the work area.

    A. 10   B. 25   C. 50   D. 100

15. All of the following are fire hazards EXCEPT flammable

    A. liquids   B. solids
    C. dusts   D. none of the above

16. Cylinder fittings should be greased

    A. weekly   B. monthly
    C. every six months   D. never

17. The presence of _____ makes materials more likely to ignite.

    A. heat   B. oxygen
    C. acetylene   D. all of the above

18. Oxygen and acetylene should be stored in _____ enclosures. 18._____

    A. locked, airtight   B. well-ventilated
    C. separate   D. air-conditioned

19. Oxygen cylinders should have _____ regulators. 19._____

    A. green   B. red   C. gray   D. black

20. Acetylene cylinders should have _____ regulators. 20._____

    A. green   B. red   C. gray   D. black

21. Oxygen regulators and hose fittings have _____ threads. 21._____

    A. right-hand   B. left-hand
    C. universal   D. all of the above

22. Acetylene regulators and hose fittings have _____ threads. 22._____

    A. left-hand   B. right-hand
    C. universal   D. all of the above

23. The oxygen cylinder should be opened _____ when preparing to begin work. 23._____

    A. one half turn   B. one full turn
    C. one and one-half turns   D. completely

24. The acetylene cylinder should be opened _____ when preparing to begin work. 24._____

    A. one half turn   B. one full turn
    C. one and one half turns   D. completely

25. To INCREASE the amount of acetylene used during an operation, 25._____

    A. gradually increase the pressure
    B. open the valve in one half turn increments
    C. use a larger diameter hose
    D. all of the above

KEY (CORRECT ANSWERS)

1.	B	11.	B
2.	A	12.	A
3.	A	13.	C
4.	B	14.	B
5.	D	15.	D
6.	A	16.	D
7.	C	17.	D
8.	B	18.	C
9.	C	19.	A
10.	C	20.	B

21. A
22. A
23. D
24. B
25. C

TEST 3

DIRECTIONS: Each question or incomplete statement is followed by several suggested answers or completions. Select the one that BEST answers the question or completes the statement. *PRINT THE LETTER OF THE CORRECT ANSWER IN THE SPACE AT THE RIGHT.*

1. Before use, the valves on both the oxygen and acetylene cylinders should be   1.____

    A. lubricated with a mineral oil
    B. wiped clean
    C. moistened with a damp cloth
    D. all of the above

2. Before attaching the regulators, both cylinder valves should be opened for an instant in order to   2.____

    A. check the pressure
    B. prime the cylinders
    C. clear any dirt blocking the valve outlets
    D. all of the above

3. Control valves on the torch should be opened   3.____

    A. before the regulators are adjusted
    B. after the regulators are adjusted
    C. to establish the desired pressures
    D. to decrease pressure when the regulator is attached

4. Of the following, the CORRECT order for removing equipment from the cylinders is   4.____

    A. close oxygen and acetylene cylinder valves, bleed hoses, open pressure adjusting screw, remove regulator
    B. open pressure adjusting screw, bleed hoses, close oxygen and acetylene cylinder valves, remove regulator
    C. close oxygen and acetylene cylinder valves, open pressure adjusting screw, bleed valves, remove regulator
    D. none of the above

5. The term *backfire* refers to   5.____

    A. the flame burning inside the torch or hoses
    B. an insufficient charge in the cylinders
    C. a torch going out unexpectedly
    D. all of the above

6. Possible causes for backfire do NOT include   6.____

    A. the nozzle tip touching the work surface
    B. a loose or dirty nozzle tip
    C. dirt on the work surface
    D. inadequate ventilation

7. The term *flashback* refers to

   A. the flame burning inside the torch or hoses
   B. an insufficient charge in the cylinders
   C. a torch going out unexpectedly
   D. an oxyacetylene induced hallucination

8. Of the following, the type of leak that is EASILY detected is an _____ leak.

   A. oxygen B. acetylene
   C. both of the above D. none of the above

9. Leaks should be checked for using a(n)

   A. electronic detector B. halide torch detector
   C. soap and water solution D. all of the above

10. An acceptable means of repairing hoses is by _____ the affected area.

    A. cutting and splicing B. taping
    C. heating D. all of the above

11. _____ tubing should NEVER be used with acetylene.

    A. Rubber B. Plastic
    C. Copper D. None of the above

12. Gas cylinders that are stored should be protected from

    A. snow B. rust
    C. direct sunlight D. all of the above

13. Oxygen cylinders should be stored AT LEAST feet from any combustible materials.

    A. 25 B. 50 C. 75 D. 100

14. Using oxyacetylene equipment in manholes or other underground structures is particularly hazardous due to

    A. poor lighting
    B. the potential build-up of flammable gas or liquids
    C. unsanitary conditions
    D. the likely presence of water

15. Of the following, the MOST care should be taken to adequately _____ underground structures.

    A. dry B. ventilate C. light D. heat

16. Liquids and gases that build up in manholes may be

    A. toxic B. suffocating
    C. flammable D. all of the above

17. If the oxygen content in a structure is below _____%, workers may not enter unless equipped with a self-contained breathing apparatus.

    A. 19.5 B. 25.5 C. 50 D. 56.5

18. Of the following, the MOST common solder used in jewelry manufacturing is 18.____

    A. gold   B. tin   C. lead   D. copper

19. When *soft soldering,* the torch flame is below _____ ° F. 19.____

    A. 600   B. 800   C. 1000   D. 1200

20. Fuel gases that are used in jewelry manufacture do NOT include 20.____

    A. propane   B. butane
    C. acetylene   D. none of the above

21. The only person REQUIRED to hold a certificate of fitness for torch operations in a jewelry manufacturing plant is the 21.____

    A. torch operator
    B. supervisor of torch operations
    C. fireguard
    D. owner of the plant

22. Fire extinguishers must be inspected every 22.____

    A. 6 months   B. year   C. two years   D. three years

23. Air for the torches used in jewelry manufacture may be supplied by all of the following means EXCEPT 23.____

    A. compressor   B. bellows
    C. mouth   D. fan

24. The certificate of fitness holder is REQUIRED to know the 24.____

    A. location and operation of all installed fire extinguishing devices
    B. location of any fire alarm stations
    C. telephone number of the fire department borough communications office
    D. all of the above

25. Fire extinguishers may contain all of the following extinguishing agents EXCEPT 25.____

    A. water   B. carbon dioxide
    C. oxygen   D. dry chemicals

KEY (CORRECT ANSWERS)

1. B
2. C
3. B
4. A
5. C

6. D
7. A
8. B
9. C
10. A

11. C
12. D
13. A
14. B
15. B

16. D
17. A
18. A
19. C
20. D

21. B
22. A
23. D
24. D
25. C

EXAMINATION SECTION
TEST 1

DIRECTIONS: Each question or incomplete statement is followed by several suggested answers or completions. Select the one that BEST answers the question or completes the statement. *PRINT THE LETTER OF THE CORRECT ANSWER IN THE SPACE AT THE RIGHT.*

1. Before splicing together the ends of two steel columns, the ends are *usually*   1._____

    A. coped B. milled C. broached D. blocked

2. Of the following heat treatment processes, the one that brings steel to the LOWEST hardness is   2._____

    A. tempering B. normalizing
    C. annealing D. nitriding

3. A riveted girder consists of flange angles, flange plates, web, and stiffeners. Of the structural members listed above, the one that would MOST likely be crimped is the   3._____

    A. flange angles B. flange plates
    C. web D. stiffeners

4. In the installation of steel studs on the flange of a beam with an automatic-end welder, the ceramic part that is removed from the stud after the completion of the welding process is known as a   4._____

    A. yoke B. batten C. collar D. ferrule

5. Of the following, the machine that should be used to make an angle from a flat plate is the   5._____

    A. shaper B. turret lathe
    C. brake D. mandrel press

6. According to the AISC Code, the MINIMUM edge distance permitted for drilled holes in structural steel plate when the edges of the plate are sheared and when 5/8" diameter bolts are to be used is   6._____

    A. 7/8" B. 1 1/8" C. 1 1/2" D. 1 3/4"

7. Of the following welding processes, the one that is presently MOST widely used in the fabrication of structural steel is _____ welding.   7._____

    A. friction B. braze C. arc D. forge

8. The COMMON fabrication practice for structural steel is to make rivet holes _____ the size of the rivet.   8._____

    A. 1/32" smaller than B. equal to
    C. 1/32" larger than D. 1/16" larger than

9. The tool that should be used to taper the top of a hole in a steel plate is a   9._____

    A. boring bar B. reamer
    C. spot facer D. countersink

61

10. The type of rivet head MOST often used for structural steel is the _____ head.

    A. truss
    B. flat
    C. button
    D. wagon box

11.

    The sketch shown above is a profile of a type of defective weld. This type of defect is known as

    A. insufficient throat
    B. overlap
    C. excessive convexity
    D. excessive concavity

12. Of the following profiles of welds shown in cross-section, the one that shows an undercut is

    A.   B.   C.   D.

13. Of the following measuring devices, the one that gives the MOST precise measurement of thickness is the

    A. micrometer caliper
    B. machinists steel scale
    C. combination square
    D. protractor

14. Of the following methods, the BEST one to use in order to check the curvature of a curved steel beam is the

    A. chord-offset
    B. radius-offset
    C. tangent-offset
    D. deflection angle-chord

15. A testing machine that measures hardness is the

    A. Riehle
    B. Tinius Olsen
    C. Scott
    D. Brinnel

16. Brittleness of steel is measured by the _____ Test.

    A. Rockwell   B. Charpy   C. Proctor   D. Spark

17. The micrometer reading shown at the right is
    A. .318"
    B. .346"
    C. .377"
    D. .392"

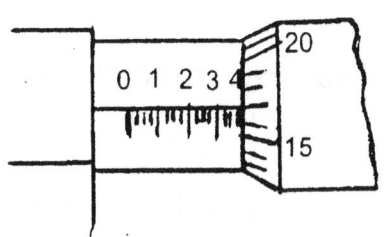

17.____

18.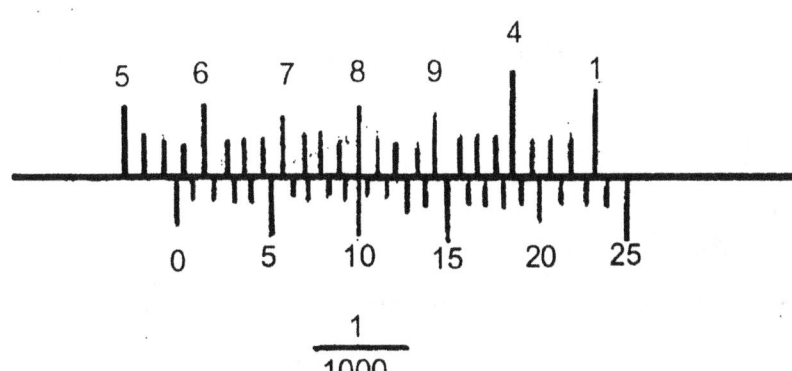

    The reading on the height gauge, with vernier shown above, is MOST NEARLY

    A. A.3.274   B. 3.560   C. 4.615   D. 4.916

18.____

19.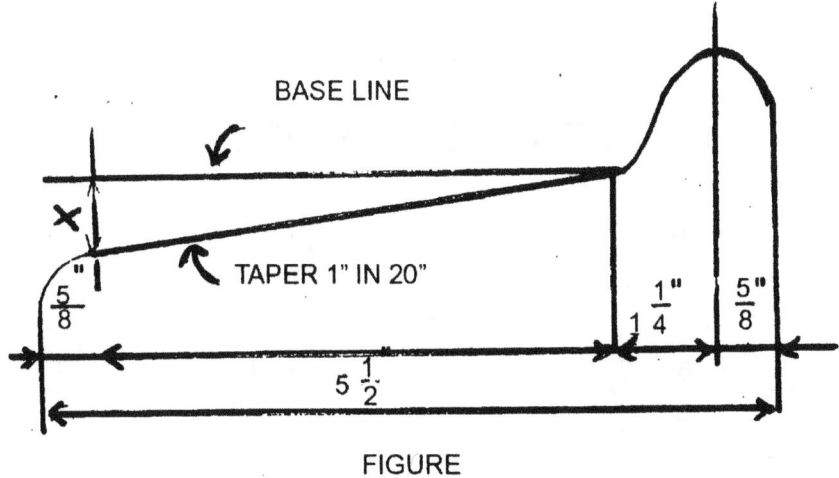

    FIGURE

    The distance X in the figure shown above is MOST NEARLY

    A. 3/32"   B. 1/8"   C. 5/32"   D. 3/16"

19.____

20. Of the following atmospheric conditions, the one under which it is MOST harmful to store welding electrodes is

    A. dampness   B. dryness   C. heat   D. cold

20.____

21. Of the following, the BEST tool to use to check the length of the circumference of the tread of a new railroad car wheel is a

    A. trammel   B. tape
    C. back-to-back gage D. protractor

21.____

22. Specifications state that the tolerance for camber of a steel beam is equal to

    $1/8" \times \dfrac{\text{total length}}{5}$

    The tolerance for camber for a beam 30 feet long is

    A. 1/2"   B. 5/8"   C. 3/4"   D. 7/8"

23. The MAIN reason for making a ladle analysis of steel is to determine the _____ of the steel.

    A. chemical composition
    B. corrosion rate
    C. fatigue limit
    D. expansion and contraction

24. The machine that is NOT used in the physical testing of steel products is the

    A. Tinnius Olsen   B. Riehle
    C. Brinnel   D. Scott

25. An electrode has a designation of E7018. The digit that designates the position or positions it is suitable for is the

    A. 7   B. 0   C. 1   D. 8

KEY (CORRECT ANSWERS)

1. B		11. C	
2. C		12. B	
3. D		13. A	
4. D		14. A	
5. C		15. D	
6. B		16. B	
7. C		17. D	
8. D		18. B	
9. D		19. C	
10. C		20. A	

21. B
22. C
23. A
24. D
25. C

TEST 2

DIRECTIONS: Each question or incomplete statement is followed by several suggested answers or completions. Select the one that BEST answers the question or completes the statement. *PRINT THE LETTER OF THE CORRECT ANSWER IN THE SPACE AT THE RIGHT.*

1. A test that is NON-DESTRUCTIVE is the _____ test.

    A. ultrasonic
    B. tensile
    C. charpy
    D. strip

2. The symbol shown below that represents the cross-section of steel is

    A. (cross-hatched)   B. (diagonal lines)   C. (horizontal lines)   D. (vertical lines)

3. The turn-of-nut method is to be used to tighten A325 bolts. The outer faces of the bolted parts are parallel to each other and perpendicular to the bolt axis (bevel washers not used). The additional required nut rotation from the *snug tight* condition is a _____ turn.

    A. 1/4   B. 1/2   C. 3/4   D. full

4. In the tensile testing of bolts, which of the following strength measurements are recorded?

    A. Yield point and ultimate strength
    B. Elastic limit and ultimate strength
    C. Yield point and fracture strength
    D. Elastic limit and fracture strength

5. In a guided bend test for weld ductility, the weld specimen is bent through an angle of

    A. 45°   B. 90°   C. 135°   D. 180°

6. The type of butt weld shown above is a double

    A. bevel   B. J   C. U   D. V

7. The conventional sign that represents a countersunk and chipped shop rivet is

    A.   B.   C.   D.

8. The structural shape represented by the designation C15 x 40 is

    A.   B.   C.   D.

9. Galvanizing of steel, when specified for grating, means coating the steel with

   A. lead   B. titanium   C. zinc   D. tin

10. The shop coat of paint MOST often specified for structural steel is

    A. vermiculite   B. red lead
    C. vinyl resin   D. latex

11. A contract states that the material in steel piles and splices shall conform to structural steel specification ASTM A36. The 36 in the specification refers to the _____ steel.

    A. thickness of the
    B. minimum length of rolled section of
    C. weight per foot of the
    D. yield point of the

12. A rectangular bar, 1 3/4" thick, must have a minimum area of .36 square inches. Of the following, the MINIMUM acceptable width of the bar is

    A. 3/32"   B. 5/32"   C. 7/32"   D. 9/32"

13. The rounded interior corners of structural steel shapes are called

    A. fillets   B. kerfs   C. dogs   D. chamfers

14. A structural steel member having a designation of 18H5 is a

    A. girt   B. purlin   C. joist   D. lintel

15. A hexagonal steel gusset plate is shown on a shop drawing with six equally spaced holes on the circumference of a 9-inch diameter circle. The distance between the centers of the adjacent holes is

    A. 4"   B. 4 1/4"   C. 4 1/2"   D. 4 3/4"

16. Shown at the right is a sketch of the top of a bolt. The marking A490 on the head of the bolt is the _____ number of the bolt.

    A. heat
    B. shipment
    C. hardness
    D. specification

Questions 17-19.

DIRECTIONS: The drawing shown below refers to Questions 17 through 19. These questions should be answered in accordance with this drawing.

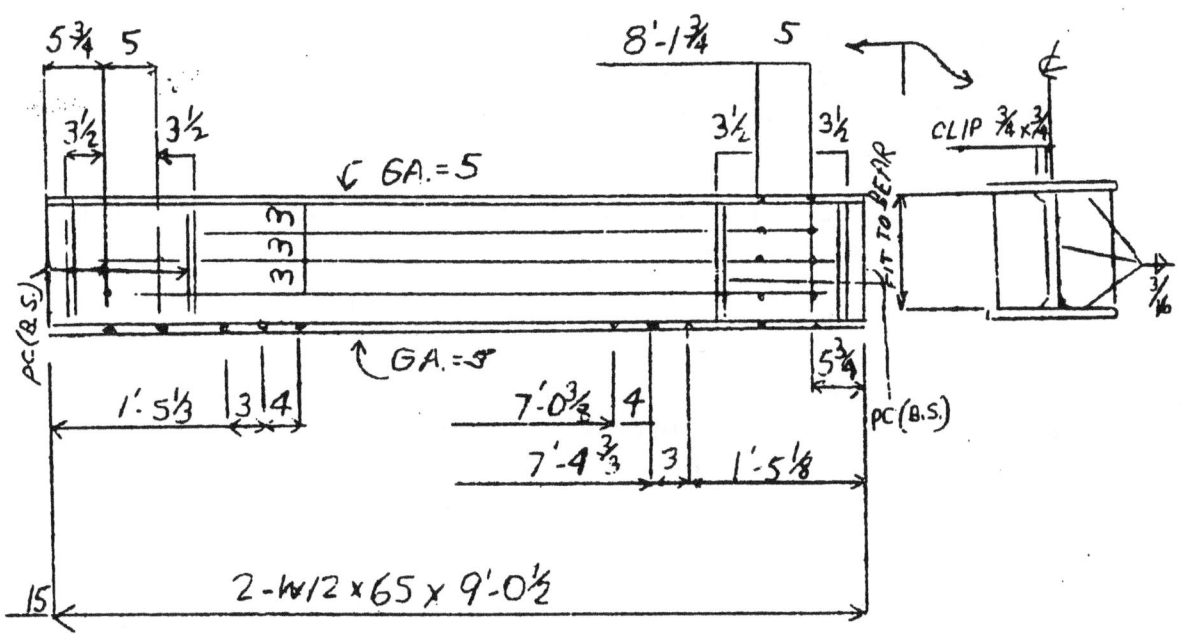

17. The welding symbol shown on the above diagram designates a _____ weld.

    A. spot B. plug C. butt D. fillet

18. The abbreviation GA. appearing on the drawing means

    A. gage B. galvanize C. gap D. gam

19. In the designation pc(B.S.) appearing on the shop drawing, the B.S. means

    A. billet steel B. bearing steel
    C. both sides D. beam stiffener

20. A specification states that in the shop assembly of structural steel, the parts of riveted structural members shall be well pinned and firmly drawn together with bolts before riveting is commenced. The pins used for aligning and holding the fabricated steel in place before bolting are known as _____ pins.

    A. linch B. drift C. clevis D. finnegan

21. Of the following items relating to a written weekly report on the status of a fabrication contract, the MOST important item is that the report should be

    A. brief B. accurate
    C. subjective D. creative

22. Of the following, in preparing a monthly report of the work inspected in a steel fabrication shop, the BEST source of data is

    A. the contract CPM diagram B. the fabricator's log book
    C. the shop drawings D. his diary

23. Of the following items, the one that is LEAST important in qualifying a steel fabricator is the number of

   A. strikes suffered by the company in the last five years
   B. paid holidays given employees
   C. years the firm has been in existence
   D. miles the plant is from the nearest railroad

24. In writing a shop accident report, it is generally BEST to make each sentence in the report _____ and with _____ idea(s).

   A. long; one
   B. long; many
   C. short; one
   D. short; many

25. A specification states that gratings which show black or uncoated spots, *dross,* improper or insufficient galvanizing or any other defects shall be rejected.
In the above specification, *dross* means

   A. dirt
   B. gloss
   C. flat
   D. clear

KEY (CORRECT ANSWERS)

1. A
2. B
3. C
4. A
5. D

6. B
7. D
8. D
9. C
10. B

11. D
12. C
13. A
14. C
15. C

16. D
17. D
18. A
19. C
20. B

21. B
22. D
23. B
24. C
25. A

EXAMINATION SECTION
TEST 1

DIRECTIONS: Directly and concisely, using brief answer form, answer the following questions.

1. Which gas does the actual cutting? 1.____
2. Why is a flux used in welding? 2.____
3. Why is a casting annealed after welding? 3.____
4. What kind of preheating flame is used in cutting? 4.____
5. Why does one crack or open the cylinder valves before connecting the regulators to the cylinders? 5.____
6. What is the BEST kind of rod to use when welding cast aluminum? 6.____
7. What material-filling rod must be used to weld together pieces of copper? 7.____
8. Of what material are welding torch tips made? 8.____
9. What metal is used to braze brass and cast iron together? 9.____
10. What do the manufactures warn welders never to use on any oxygen connections? 10.____

2 (#1)

KEY (CORRECT ANSWERS)

1. Oxygen

2. Clean
   Make metal flow

3. Prevent hardening (keep soft) (relieve strains)

4. Neutral flame

5. Blow out dust (clean)

6. Cast aluminum (aluminum)

7. Copper

8. Copper

9. Bronze (Tobin bronze)

10. Oil
    Grease

TEST 2

DIRECTIONS: Directly and concisely, using brief answer form, answer the following questions.

1. What is the purpose of preheating? 1.____
2. What is the flame called that is caused by an excess of oxygen at the torch? 2.____
3. What is the flame called that results from a proper amount of both acetylene and oxygen? 3.____
4. What kind of flame is used for welding steel? 4.____
5. What chemical is mixed with water to form acetylene gas? 5.____
6. What is the BEST kind of flux to use on brass? 6.____
7. What is the BEST kind of flux to use on brass? 7.____
8. In welding unlike metals, of which metal is the welding rod usually made? 8.____
9. What kind of flame is used for burning? 9.____
10. What is the flame called that is caused by an excess of acetylene at the torch? 10.____

KEY (CORRECT ANSWERS)

1. Prevent cracking (take care of expansion)

2. Oxidizing flame

3. Neutral flame

4. Reducing
   Neutral
   Carbonizing

5. Calcium carbide (carbide)

6. Borax

7. Dirty tip
   Tip too hot
   Lack of pressure
   Wrong mixture
   Touch metal

8. One with lower melting point
   Softer
   Bronze
   Brass

9. Preheating
   Oxidizing

10. Reducing (carbonizing) flame

TEST 3

DIRECTIONS: Directly and concisely, using brief answer form, answer the following questions.

1. At the present time, what class of metals are the only ones that can be cut by the oxy-acetylene process? 1.____

2. What kind of rod is used when welding malleable iron castings? 2.____

3. What material, besides acetylene gas, is in the acetylene tank? 3.____

4. What is the danger in using grease or oil on oxygen connections? 4.____

5. What material almost never requires a flux during welding? 5.____

6. Below what thickness can metal sheets be welded without the use of a welding rod? 6.____

7. What is used to line up crankshafts before welding? 7.____

8. What method is used on light castings to put the flux on the weld? 8.____

9. In what way can one tell by looking at the hot metal that too much oxygen is being used in welding? 9.____

10. What is put in the acetylene tank to prevent explosion? 10.____

KEY (CORRECT ANSWERS)

1. Ferrous metals (iron, steel)

2. Bronze
   Brass

3. Asbestos
   Acetone

4. Explosion (combustion) (fire)

5. Steel (low carbon steel)

6. 1/16 to 1/8 of an inch

7. Vee blocks

8. Dip rod in flux

9. Boil (foam)
   Spark (burn)
   White (shiny)

10. Asbestos
    Acetone

TEST 4

DIRECTIONS: Directly and concisely, using brief answer form, answer the following questions.

1. What determines the amount of current to be used? 1.____
2. What polarity electrode is used to make the rod melt faster? 2.____
3. Name two nonferrous metals that can be welded electrically? 3.____
4. What is the rod called that has a low carbon content? 4.____
5. What effect does holding the electrode against the material have on the arc? 5.____
6. What is the test called which determines the strength of the weld? 6.____
7. What polarity should be used in welding nonferrous metals with metal electrodes? 7.____
8. What pole is used on the electrode for reverse polarity? 8.____
9. How many line wires are used on a three-phase, 440-volt welding machine? 9.____
10. What polarity should the electrode be when welding with a carbon arc on direct current? 10.____

KEY (CORRECT ANSWERS)

1. Thickness (size) of metal (work) (material) Size of rod (electrode)

2. Reverse (positive) (plus)

3. Bronze
   Aluminum
   Brass
   Copper
   Monel
   Stainless steel

4. Mild (soft) electrode
   Low carbon rod

5. Kills (freezes) (sticks)
   Grounds (shorts) (stops)

6. Tensile (pull) test

7. Reverse (positive) (plus)

8. Positive (plus)

9. Three

10. Negative (straight) (direct) (standard)

TEST 5

DIRECTIONS: Directly and concisely, using brief answer form, answer the following questions.

1. What term is applied to the strip or block used to prevent molten metal from running through the joint? 1.____
2. What other name is there for the welding rod? 2.____
3. In a longitudinal pipe weld, what is done to the work to prevent distortion? 3.____
4. What kind of electrodes are usually used for cutting? 4.____
5. Which type of welding machine has no rotating parts? 5.____
6. Name the MOST common cause of insufficient penetration. 6.____
7. Why is metallic arc welding generally faster than oxyacetylene? 7.____
8. Which end of the arc is the hottest? 8.____
9. What should be done to electrical connections before starting to weld? 9.____
10. On nonferrous metals, which side of the machine is used on the electrode? 10.____

2 (#5)

KEY (CORRECT ANSWERS)

1. Backing (back-up) strip

2. Electrode

3. Stagger (spot) (tack) (step) weld
   Clamp (reinforce) it to stiff back
   Wedge (spread) open

4. Carbon
   Shielded (coated)

5. A.C. (jazz box) (juice box) (transformer)

6. Not enough heat (voltage) (amperage) (current)
   Too much speed

7. Hot (no preheating) (faster penetration)

8. Positive (plus)
   Jumping-off point
   Work end (material) (metal)

9. Tighten
   Clean

10. Reverse (positive) (plus)

TEST 6

DIRECTIONS: Directly and concisely, using brief answer form, answer the following questions.

1. What is the cup-shaped cavity called that is made by the welding rod? 1.____
2. What should be done to manganese steel immediately after welding? 2.____
3. What other arc is used in electric welding besides the metallic arc? 3.____
4. What term describes the type of welding when the welding rod is not manipulated by hand? 4.____
5. Why does one stud a cast-iron weld? 5.____
6. When welding mild steel with bare electrodes, what side of the welding current should the work be on? 6.____
7. What size electrode is used to weld metal 1/8 inch thick? 7.____
8. What element from the air does the coating on the electrode prevent from entering the weld? 8.____
9. What should be done to the edges of thick plates to prepare them for welding? 9.____
10. When welding stainless steel, what adjustment is made for polarity? 10.____

KEY (CORRECT ANSWERS)

1. Crater (crevice) (cradle) (pocket)

2. Quench (chill) (cool)
   Peen (hammer) (pound)

3. Carbon arc

4. Automatic (machine)

5. To make better bond (strength) (hold)

6. Straight (plus) (positive)

7. 3/32 to 5/32 inch

8. Oxygen
   Nitrogen

9. Bevel (chamfer) ("V") (taper)

10. Reverse

ARITHMETICAL REASONING
EXAMINATION SECTION
TEST 1

DIRECTIONS: Each question or incomplete statement is followed by several suggested answers or completions. Select the one that BEST answers the question or completes the statement. *PRINT THE LETTER OF THE CORRECT ANSWER IN THE SPACE AT THE RIGHT.*

1. A custodial assistant takes an average of forty minutes to mop 1,000 square feet of floor. The amount of time this custodial assistant should take to mop the floor of a rectangular corridor eight feet wide by sixty feet long is, on the average, MOST NEARLY _____ minutes.

    A. 10 B. 20 C. 30 D. 40

2. An auditorium eighty feet by 100 feet must be swept in one hour.
If each custodial assistant takes fifteen minutes to sweep 1,000 square feet of auditorium area, the number of custodial assistants that must be assigned to complete the sweeping in one hour is

    A. 1 B. 2 C. 3 D. 4

3. A detergent manufacturer recommends mixing 8 ounces of detergent in one gallon of water to prepare a cleaning solution.
The amount of the same detergent which should be mixed with thirty gallons of water to obtain the same strength cleaning solution is _____ ounces.

    A. 24 B. 30 C. 240 D. 380

4. The floor area of a corridor 8 feet wide and 72 feet long is MOST NEARLY _____ square feet.

    A. 80 B. 420 C. 580 D. 870

5. A water tank that is 5 feet in diameter and 30 feet high has a volume of MOST NEARLY _____ cubic feet.

    A. 150 B. 250 C. 600 D. 1,200

6. The circumference of a circle with a radius of 5 inches is MOST NEARLY _____ inches.

    A. 31.3 B. 30.0 C. 20.1 D. 13.4

7. Suppose that you are the custodian-engineer and an employee works for you at the rate of $8.70 per hour with time and one-half paid for time worked after 40 hours in one week. His gross pay for working 53 hours in one week is MOST NEARLY

    A. $461.10 B. $482.10 C. $487.65 D. $517.65

8. Suppose that you are the custodian-engineer and one of your employees has gotten gross earnings of $437.10 for the week, all of which is subject to deductions at the rate of 4.8%.
   The amount which should be deducted from the employee's gross earnings for the week is MOST NEARLY

   A. $2.10   B. $14.70   C. $17.70   D. $20.97

9. The directions on the label of a bottle of detergent call for mixing four ounces of detergent with one gallon of water to make a cleaning solution for washing floors. In order to obtain a larger amount of solution of the same strength, one quart of the detergent should be mixed with _____ gallons of water.

   A. 2   B. 4   C. 6   D. 8

10. The area of a lawn which is 58 feet wide by 96 feet long is MOST NEARLY _____ square feet.

    A. 5,000   B. 5,500   C. 6,000   D. 6,500

11. In a building which is heated by an oil-fired boiler, 2,100 gallons of fuel oil were burned in a period in which the degree days reached a total of 1,400.
    If all other conditions remained constant, the number of gallons of fuel oil that would be burned in this building during a period in which the degree days reached a total of 3,600 is

    A. 2,400   B. 2,900   C. 4,800   D. 5,400

12. The instructions for mixing a powdered cleaner in water state, *Mix three ounces of powder in a 14-quart pail three-quarters full of water.* A cleaner asks you how much powdered cleaner he should use in a mop truck containing 28 gallons of water to obtain the same strength solution.
    The CORRECT answer is _____ ounces of powder.

    A. 6   B. 8   C. 24   D. 32

13. A custodian-engineer wishes to order sponges in the most economical manner. Keeping in mind that large sponges can be cut up into many smaller sizes, the one of the following that has the LEAST cost per cubic inch of sponge is

    A. 2" x 4" x 6" sponges @ $.48
    B. 4" x 8" x 12" sponges @ $2.88
    C. 4" x 6" x 36" sponges @ $9.60
    D. 6" x 8" x 32" sponges @ $19.20

14. Two cleaners swept four corridors in 24 minutes. Each corridor measured 12 feet x 176 feet.
    The space swept per man per minute was MOST NEARLY _____ square feet.

    A. 50   B. 90   C. 180   D. 350

15. Kerosene costs 60 cents a quart.
    At that rate, two gallons would cost

    A. $2.40   B. $3.60   C. $4.80   D. $6.00

16. The instructions on a container of cleaning compound states, *Mix one pound of compound in 5 gallons of water.* Using these instructions, the amount of compound which should be added to 15 quarts of water is MOST likely _____ ounces.

    A. 3   B. 8   C. 12   D. 48

17. Suppose that you are the custodian-engineer and one of your employees has gross earnings of $582.80 for the week, all of which is subject to Social Security deductions at the rate of 4.8%.
    The amount which should be deducted from the employee's gross earnings for the week is MOST NEARLY

    A. $2.80   B. $19.60   C. $23.60   D. $27.96

18. Suppose that you are a custodian-engineer and an employee works for you at the rate of $11.60 per hour with time and one-half paid for time worked after 40 hours in one week. His gross pay for working 53 hours in one week is MOST NEARLY

    A. $614.80   B. $642.80   C. $650.20   D. $690.20

19. The volume, in cubic feet, of a cylindrical tank 6 feet in diameter x 35 feet long is MOST NEARLY

    A. 210   B. 990   C. 1,260   D. 3,960

20. A room 12 feet wide by 25 feet long has a floor area of _____ square feet.

    A. 37   B. 200   C. 300   D. 400

21. How many hours will it take a worker to sweep a floor space of 2,800 square feet if he sweeps at the rate of 800 square feet per hour?

    A. 8   B. 6 1/2   C. 3 1/2   D. 2 1/2

22. One gallon of water contains

    A. 2 quarts   B. 4 quarts   C. 2 pints   D. 4 pints

23. A standard cleaning solution is prepared by mixing 4 ounces of detergent powder in 2 gallons of water.
    The number of ounces of detergent powder needed for the same strength solution in 5 gallons of water is

    A. 4   B. 6   C. 8   D. 10

24. The ceiling of a room which measures 20 feet x 30 feet is to be given two coats of paint. If one gallon of paint will cover 500 square feet, the two coats of paint will require a MINIMUM of _____ gallons.

    A. 1.5   B. 2   C. 2.4   D. 3.2

25. The floor area of a room which measures 10 feet long by 10 feet wide is _____ square feet.

    A. 20   B. 40   C. 100   D. 1,000

KEY (CORRECT ANSWERS)

1.	B		11.	D
2.	B		12.	D
3.	C		13.	B
4.	C		14.	C
5.	C		15.	C
6.	A		16.	C
7.	D		17.	D
8.	D		18.	D
9.	D		19.	B
10.	B		20.	C

21. C
22. B
23. D
24. C
25. C

SOLUTIONS TO PROBLEMS

1. $(8')(60') = 480$ sq.ft. Let x = required time in minutes.
   Then, $\dfrac{40}{1000} = \dfrac{x}{480}$. Solving, x = 19.2 or nearly 20.

2. $(80')(100') = 8000$ sq.ft. Each custodian can sweep $(1000)(4) = 4000$ sq.ft. in 1 hour. Then, $8000 \div 4000 = 2$.

3. $(8)(30) = 240$ ounces

4. $(8')(72') = 576$ sq.ft. or nearly 580 sq.ft.

5. Volume $= (\pi)(2.5')^2(30') \approx 589$ cu.ft. or nearly 600 cu.ft.

6. Circumference $= (2\pi)(5") \approx 31.3$ sq.in.

7. $(\$8.70)(40) + (\$13.05)(13) = \$517.65$

8. $(\$437.10)(.048) \approx \$20.97$

9. 1 quart = 32 oz. Then, $32 \div 4 = 8$ gallons of water

10. $(58')(96') = 5568$ sq.ft., which is closest to 5500 sq.ft.

11. Let x = number of gallons. Then, $\dfrac{2100}{1400} = \dfrac{x}{3600}$. Solving, x = 5400

12. $(.75)(14)(.25) = 2.625$ gallons of water. Let x = number of ounces of powder needed. Then, $\dfrac{3}{2.625} = \dfrac{x}{28}$. Solving, x = 32

13. For selection B, $(4")(8")(12") = 384$ cu.in., and the cost per cubic inch $= \$2.88 \div 384 = \$.0075$. This is lower than selections A ($.01), C ($.011), or D ($.015).

14. Two men sweep $(4)(12')(176') = 8448$ total sq.ft. in 24 min. = 352 sq.ft. per min. Each man sweeps 176 sq.ft. per min $\approx$ 180 sq.ft. per min.

15. Two gallons = 8 quarts. Then, $(\$.60)(8) = \$4.80$

16. 15 quarts = 3.75 gallons of water. Let x = required number of ounces of compound. Then, $\dfrac{16}{5} = \dfrac{x}{3.75}$. Solving, x = 12

17. $(\$582.80)(.048) \approx \$27.96$

18. $(\$11.60 \times 40) + (\$17.40)(13) = \$690.20$

19. Volume $= (\pi)(3')^2(35') \approx 990$ cu.ft.

20. (12')(25') = 300 sq.ft.

21. 2800 ÷ 800 = 3 1/2 hours

22. One gallon = 4 quarts

23. Let x = required number of ounces. Then, $\frac{4}{2} = \frac{x}{5}$. Solving, x = 10

24. 2 coats means (2)(20')(30') = 1200 sq.ft. Then, 1200 ÷ 500 = 2.4 gallons

25. (10')(10') = 100 sq.ft.

TEST 2

DIRECTIONS: Each question or incomplete statement is followed by several suggested answers or completions. Select the one that BEST answers the question or completes the statement. *PRINT THE LETTER OF THE CORRECT ANSWER IN THE SPACE AT THE RIGHT.*

1. Assume that a certain elevator starter is at work 8 hours a day, which includes 1 hour for lunch and two 15-minute relief periods. The rest of the workday the starter is performing his duties.
   If the starter works 4 days, the TOTAL amount of time the starter will actually be performing his duties is _____ hours.

   A. 24   B. 26   C. 28   D. 32

   1.____

2. Assume that a certain bank of 18 elevators operating at full capacity could move 3,240 passengers an hour from the main lobby.
   The number of passengers that one of these elevators could move from the lobby every 15 minutes is, on the average,

   A. 12   B. 22   C. 45   D. 180

   2.____

3. In a certain agency, the amount of absence due to injury or illness was an average of 6 hours a month for each employee.
   If this agency had 335 employees, the TOTAL number of hours lost in a year due to injury or sickness was

   A. 4,020   B. 20,100   C. 24,120   D. 28,140

   3.____

4. Assume that in a certain building the elevators must handle 16% of the building population during a peak traffic period.
   If the building population is 2,825, the TOTAL number of people the elevators must handle during a peak traffic period is

   A. 396   B. 424   C. 436   D. 452

   4.____

5. From his coin bank, a boy took 3 half dollars, 8 quarters, 7 dimes, 6 nickels, and 9 pennies to deposit in his school savings account.
   Express in dollars and cents the TOTAL amount of money he deposited.

   A. $2.82   B. $4.59   C. $6.42   D. $7.52

   5.____

6. If a roast that requires 1 hour and 40 minutes of roasting time has been in the oven for 55 minutes, how many more minutes of roasting time are required?

   A. 30   B. 36   C. 45   D. 55

   6.____

7. On the first day of its drive, a school raised $40, which was 33 1/3% of its Red Cross quota.
   How much was the quota?

   A. $120   B. $130   C. $140   D. $150

   7.____

8. When 0.750 is divided by 0.875, the answer is MOST NEARLY

   A. 0.250   B. 0.312   C. 0.624   D. 0.857

   8.____

9. The circumference of a 6-inch diameter circle is MOST NEARLY _____ feet.

   A. 1.57   B. 2.1   C. 2.31   D. 4.24

10. An 18" piece of cable that weighs 3 pounds per foot has a total weight of _____ pounds.

    A. 5.5   B. 4.5   C. 3.0   D. 1.5

11. The sum of 0.135, 0.040, 0.812, and 0.961 is

    A. 1.424   B. 1.625   C. 1.843   D. 1.948

12. If an elevator carries a load of 1,600 pounds uniformly distributed on a 4 feet by 5 feet floor, the weight per square foot is _____ pounds.

    A. 98   B. 80   C. 65   D. 40

13. If one cubic inch of lead weighs one-quarter of a pound, the weight of a bar of lead 1" high by 2" wide by 8" long is _____ pounds.

    A. 1.8   B. 2.5   C. 3.1   D. 4

14. Assume that 8 mechanics have been assigned to do a job that must be finished in 5 days. At the end of 3 days, the men have completed only half the job.
    In order to complete the job on time in the remaining 2 days, the MINIMUM number of extra men that should be assigned is

    A. 2   B. 3   C. 4   D. 6

15. An elevator supply manufacturer quotes a list price of $625 less 10 and 5 percent for ten contactors.
    The actual cost for these ten contactors is MOST NEARLY

    A. $562   B. $554   C. $534   D. $522

16. To find the largest number of passengers, including the operator, allowed to ride in an elevator, divide the rated capacity of the elevator by 150.
    According to this rule, what is the LARGEST number of passengers NOT counting the operator that may be carried in an elevator with a rated capacity of 3,000 lbs.?

    A. 18   B. 19   C. 20   D. 21

17. Suppose that the work schedule for operators is 5 days a week, 8 hours a day.
    In a period of 4 weeks, with no holidays, how many hours will you be required to be on duty?

    A. 160   B. 180   C. 200   D. 225

18. Mr. Jones takes $200 to cover his expenses for a week. He spends $6.00 for carfare coming to work and $6.00 for carfare going home. He buys a $1 newspaper each day and spends $16.00 for lunch and $5.00 for cigarettes each day.
    How much money does he have left at the end of a 5-day work week?

    A. $30.00   B. $55.00   C. $100.00   D. $170.00

3 (#2)

19. Twelve hundred employees work in an office building.
Twenty percent of these employees work on the 4th floor and 25% work on the 5th floor.
The TOTAL number of employees who work on the 4th and 5th floors together is

   A. 240   B. 300   C. 540   D. 660

20. An elevator makes one roundtrip every 5 minutes, on the average.
How many roundtrips does it make between 8:15 A.M. and 9:45 A.M.?

   A. 12   B. 18   C. 20   D. 22

21. The floor of an elevator car measures 7 feet by 8 feet 6 inches.
How many square feet of linoleum would be needed to cover this floor?

   A. 31   B. 42   C. 59 1/2   D. 62 1/2

Questions 22-25.

   DIRECTIONS: Each question consists of a statement. You are to indicate whether the statement is TRUE (T) or FALSE (F).

22. In a city building, there are 20 elevators. If on one day five percent of the elevators are out of order, the number of elevators out of order is 2.

23. An elevator operator puts in 32 hours of overtime in January, 26 hours in February, 10 hours in March, 10 hours in April, and 27 hours in May. The average amount of overtime this operator worked per month for these five months is 21 hours.

24. A large city building normally has 45 elevator operators on its day shift. The vacation rules require that only 1/5 be allowed away at any time. The number of operators that may be on vacation at one time is nine.

25. In a six-story city building, there are 13 offices on the first floor, 19 offices on the second floor, 18 offices on the third floor, 17 offices on the fourth floor, 21 offices on the fifth floor, and 23 offices on the sixth floor. The total number of offices in this building is 109.

KEY (CORRECT ANSWERS)

1. B
2. C
3. C
4. D
5. B

6. C
7. A
8. D
9. A
10. B

11. D
12. B
13. D
14. C
15. C

16. B
17. A
18. A
19. C
20. B

21. C
22. F
23. T
24. T
25. F

5 (#2)

SOLUTIONS TO PROBLEMS

1. 4(8-1-.5) = 26 hours

2. Each elevator can move 3240 ÷ 18 = 180 passengers per hour, which = 45 passengers per 15 minutes.

3. (335)(6)(12) = 24,120 hours per year.

4. (2825)(.16) = 452

5. (3)(.50) + (8)(.25) + (7)(.10) + (6)(.05) + (9)(.01) = $4.59

6. 1 hr. 40 min. - 55 min. = 100 min. - 55 min. = 45 min.

7. $40 ÷ $33\frac{1}{3}$% = $40 ÷ $\frac{1}{3}$ = $120

8. .750 ÷ .875 ≈ .857

9. Circumference = ($\frac{1}{2}$')(π) ≈ 1.57'

10. 18" ÷ 12" = 1.5. Then, (1.5)(3) = 4.5 lbs.

11. .135 + .040 + .812 + .961 = 1.948

12. (4')(5') = 20 sq.ft. Then, 1600 ÷ 20 = 80 lbs. per sq.ft.

13. (1")(2")(8") = 16 cu.in. Then, (16)(1/4) = 4 pounds

14. 8 men x 3 cars = 50% of work; 24 man-days = 50% of work; 48 man-days = 100%; 24 man-days ÷ 2 days = 12 men per day = 4 extra men

15. ($625)(.90)(.95) ≈ $534

16. 3000 ÷ 150 = 20 people, including the operator. Thus, only 19 passengers are allowed.

17. (8)(5)(4) = 160 hours

18. $200 - 5($6.00+$6.00+$1+$16.00+$5.00) = $30.00

19. (1200)(20%+25%) = (1200)(.45) = 540

20. 9:45 AM - 8:15 AM = 90 min. Then, 90 ÷ 5 = 18 roundtrips

21. (7')(8 1/2') = 59 1/2 sq.ft.

22. False; (20)(.05) = 1, not 2.

23. True. (32+26+10+10+27) ÷ 5 = 21

24. True. (45)(1/5) = 9

25. False. 13 + 19 + 18 + 17 + 21 + 23 = 111, not 109

TEST 3

DIRECTIONS: Each question or incomplete statement is followed by several suggested answers or completions. Select the one that BEST answers the question or completes the statement. *PRINT THE LETTER OF THE CORRECT ANSWER IN THE SPACE AT THE RIGHT.*

1. When 60,987 is added to 27,835, the answer is 1.____
   A. 80,712   B. 80,822   C. 87,712   D. 88,822

2. The sum of 693 + 787 + 946 + 355 + 731 is 2.____
   A. 3,512   B. 3,502   C. 3,412   D. 3,402

3. When 2,586 is subtracted from 3,003, the answer is 3.____
   A. 417   B. 527   C. 1,417   D. 1,527

4. When 1.32 is subtracted from 52.6, the answer is 4.____
   A. 3.94   B. 5.128   C. 39.4   D. 51.28

5. When 56 is multiplied by 438, the answer is 5.____
   A. 840   B. 4,818   C. 24,528   D. 48,180

6. When 8.7 is multiplied by .34, the answer is MOST NEARLY 6.____
   A. 2.9   B. 3.0   C. 29.5   D. 29.6

7. When 1/2 is divided by 2/3, the answer is 7.____
   A. 1/3   B. 3/4   C. 1 1/3   D. 3

8. When 8,340 is divided by 38, the answer is MOST NEARLY 8.____
   A. 210   B. 218   C. 219   D. 220

9. Assume that a helper earns $11.16 an hour and that he works 250 seven-hour days a year. 9.____
   His gross yearly salary will be
   A. $19,430   B. $19,530   C. $19,650   D. $19,780

10. On a certain map, a distance of 10 miles is represented by 1/2 inch. 10.____
    If two towns are 3 1/2 inches apart on this map, express, in miles, the actual distance between the two towns.
    A. 70   B. 80   C. 90   D. 100

11. The area of the triangle shown at the right is _____ square inches. 11.____
    A. 120
    B. 240
    C. 360
    D. 480

12. The sum of 1/3 + 2/5 + 5/6 is   12.____

   A. 1 17/30   B. 1 3/5   C. 1 5/8   D. 1 5/6

13. The sum of the following dimensions, 3'2 1/4", 0'8 7/8", 2'6 3/8", 2'9 3/4", and 1'0", is   13.____

   A. 9'2 7/8"   B. 10'3 1/4"
   C. 10'7 3/7"   D. 11'4 1/4"

14. If the scale of a drawing is 1/8" to the foot, then a 1/2" measurement on the drawing would represent an actual length of _____ feet.   14.____

   A. 2   B. 4   C. 8   D. 16

15. Assume that an area measures 78 feet by 96 feet. The number of square feet in this area is   15.____

   A. 7,478   B. 7,488   C. 7,498   D. 7,508

16. If a can of paint costs $17.50, four dozen cans of this paint will cost   16.____

   A. $837.50   B. $840.00   C. $842.50   D. $845.00

17. The number of square feet in 1 square yard is   17.____

   A. 3   B. 6   C. 9   D. 12

18. The sum of 4 1/2 inches, 3 1/4 inches, and 7 1/2 inches is 1 foot _____ inches.   18.____

   A. 3   B. 3 1/4   C. 3 1/2   D. 4

19. If a room is 10 feet by 18 feet, the number of square feet of floor space in it is   19.____

   A. 1,800   B. 180   C. 90   D. 28

20. A jacket that was marked at $12.50 was sold for $10. What was the rate of discount on the marked price?   20.____

   A. 10%   B. 15%   C. 18%   D. 20%

Questions 21-25.

DIRECTIONS: Each question consists of a statement. You are to indicate whether the statement is TRUE (T) or FALSE (F).

21. Three-eighths (3/8") of an inch is equivalent to .0375".   21.____

22. A floor measuring 12 feet by 9 feet contains 36 sq.ft.   22.____

23. A box measuring 18 inches square and 16 inches deep will have a volume of 36 cubic feet.   23.____

24. If the charge for a long distance telephone call is 50¢ for the first 5 minutes and 7¢ for each minute after that, then for 85¢ a person could speak for 10 minutes.   24.____

25. If 15 gallons of gasoline cost $14.85 and you use up 10 gallons, then the value of the gasoline which is still left is $4.95.   25.____

KEY (CORRECT ANSWERS)

1. D
2. A
3. A
4. D
5. C

6. B
7. B
8. C
9. B
10. A

11. A
12. A
13. B
14. B
15. B

16. B
17. C
18. B
19. B
20. D

21. F
22. F
23. F
24. T
25. T

SOLUTIONS TO PROBLEMS

1. 60,987 + 27,835 = 88,822

2. 693 + 787 + 946 + 355 + 731 = 3512

3. 3003 - 2586 = 417

4. 52.6 - 1.32 = 51.28

5. (56)(438) = 24,528

6. (8.7)(.34) = 2.958 ≈ 3.0

7. $\frac{1}{2} \div \frac{2}{3} = \frac{1}{2} \cdot \frac{3}{2} = \frac{3}{4}$

8. 8340 ÷ 38 ≈ 219.47 ≈ 219

9. ($11.16)(7)(250) = $19,530

10. 3 1/2" ÷ 1/2" = 7. Then, (7)(10) = 70 miles

11. Area = (1/2)(10")(24") = 120 sq.in.

12. $\frac{1}{3} + \frac{2}{5} + \frac{5}{6} = \frac{10}{30} + \frac{12}{30} + \frac{25}{30} = \frac{47}{30} = 1\frac{17}{30}$

13. 3'2 1/4" + 0'8 7/8" + 2'6 3/8" + 2'9 3/4" + 1'0" = 8'25 18/8" = 10'3 1/4"

14. 1/2" ÷ 1/8" = 4. Then, (4)(1 ft.) = 4 ft.

15. (78')(96') = 7488 sq.ft.

16. (48)($17.50) = $840.00

17. 1 sq.yd. = (3)(3) = 9 sq.ft.

18. 4 1/2" + 3 1/4" + 7 1/2" = 14 5/4" = 1 foot 3 1/4 inches

19. (10')(18') = 180 sq.ft.

20. $12.50 - $10 = $2.50. Then, $2.50 ÷ $12.50 = .20 = 20%

21. False. 3/8" = .375", not .0375"

22. False. (12')(9') = 108 sq.ft., not 36 sq.ft.

23. False. (18")(18")(16") = 5184 cu.in. = 3 cu.ft., not 36 cu.ft.
    Note: 1 cu.ft. = 1728 cu.in.

24. True. The cost for 10 minutes = .50 + (.07)(10-5) = .85

25. True. $14.85 ÷ 15 = $.99 per gallon. The value of 5 gallons = (5)($.99) = $4.95

PRINCIPLES AND PRACTICES OF OCCUPATIONAL SAFETY AND HEALTH IN WELDING

TABLE OF CONTENTS

	Page
I. Welding Defined	1
II. Health and Safety Problems	1
Why Welding Problems Vary	1
Basic Hazards	1
1. Infrared and Ultra-Violet Radiation	1
2. Contact with Hot Metal or Sparks	1
3. Metal Fumes and Gases	2
4. Accidents from Material Handling	2
5. Shock from Electrical Current	2
III. Controlling the Hazards	2
IV. Management Responsibilities	3
V. Responsibility of Workers	3

PRINCIPLES AND PRACTICES OF OCCUPATIONAL SAFETY AND HEALTH IN WELDING

I. WELDING DEFINED

Welding is a method of joining two metal surfaces by fusing the contacted surfaces. There are about 40 different types of welding processes in use commercially. Some of the more popular types of welding processes include
   a. oxygen-acetylene welding,
   b. helium arc welding,
   c. carbon arc welding,
   d. resistance welding,
   e. metal electrode arc welding, and
   f. brazing operations.

The industrial welding process may be shielded to prevent oxidation and may be completely automatic as with the use of welding machines.

II. HEALTH AND SAFETY PROBLEMS

There are several potential health and safety problems associated with welding. However, with properly instituted precautionary measures and work procedures, there need be no danger to the health and safety of the welder.

WHY WELDING PROBLEMS VARY

Welding problems will vary with the methods of welding, location of work, materials being welded, and the instituted control measures.

BASIC HAZARDS

Certain hazards are common to most welding processes. Principally, these are damage to the eyes and skin from infrared and ultraviolet radiation, burns from contact with hot metal or sparks, adverse physiological effects from breathing metal fumes and gases, accidents from material handling, and shock from electric current.

1. *Infrared and Ultra-Violet Radiation*

    Blinding light is a familiar observation of a welding process. Molten metal manifests infrared radiation, the electric arc produces ultraviolet radiation, and the total operation generates intense visible light.

    Glare and radiation are a problem to the welder; they also present severe problems to the welder's helper who often lacks normal protective equipment such as goggles and proper clothing.

2. *Contact with Hot Metal or Sparks*

    Sudden and pulsating flashes can result in "flash burns" to the eyes. Eye burns are very painful and repeated exposure can cause permanent eye damage.

    Intense radiant energy may also cause skin damage and can cause cotton clothing to deteriorate.

    Woolen or leather garments are normally recommended for welders as affording better protection from sparks and fire as well as being more durable. Welding helmets, gloves, goggles of proper type, and other items of protective clothing, are available for providing protection to welders.

3. *Metal Fumes and Gases*

   The potential harm from gases and fumes generated by a welding operation depends upon the chemical composition of the fume, the concentration in the breathing zone, and the length of worker exposure.

   The composition of the fume is determined by the various materials involved in the welding process and by the temperature of the welding operation. The more important air contaminants that may be involved are ozone, carbon dioxide, carbon monoxide, the oxides of nitrogen, and the various specific constituents of the rods, rod coatings, and the metal themselves.

   The oxides of nitrogen and ozone are the principal toxic gases produced by welding on steel. Ozone, an intensely irritating gas, is produced by the action of the electric arc. Other toxic fumes may be generated if the steel has been coated with various materials or on alloys containing certain materials. Some non-toxic paints may produce toxic fumes when heated under the welding torch. For example, certain phthalic-base paints may give off extremely irritating fumes. Fumes from metals such as copper and zinc are cable of producing metal fume fever. Metal fume fever is self-limiting and is never known to be fatal; however, the distress and discomfort are quite objectionable and for this reason exposure should be controlled.

4. *Accidents from Material Handling*

   Most welding is done with coated rods or electrodes. Compounds which are contained in welding rod coatings include oxides of various metals, hydroxides, carbonates, silicates, fluorides, and organic materials. The fluorides are of the greatest significance because of their toxicity and because large amounts are released during welding. The coatings on welding rods used for stainless steel are invariably high in fluorides, and requires strict controls. Fluorides are also present in the fluxes used in some types of welding, brazing, or soldering. Certain of the fluxes used for silver solders contain cadmium, which can produce toxic fumes causing a chemical pneumonitis in man. The welding of alloys, particularly those containing beryllium, can be exceptionally hazardous. Beryllium and its compounds can cause lung disease and certain skin conditions.

5. *Shock from Electrical Current*

   The avoidance of electric shock is largely within the control of the welder. Most electric shocks experienced at welding voltages have not caused severe injury; however, these voltages are sufficiently high that under certain conditions they may be lethal. Even mild shocks can produce involuntary muscle contractions leading to injurious falls sometimes from high places. The severity of the shock is determined largely by the path of the current and the amount flowing through the body; this is determined by the voltage and the contact resistance of the area of skin involved. Wearing clothing damp from perspiration or working in wet conditions reduces skin contact resistance and thus increases the risk of electric shock.

III. CONTROLLING THE HAZARDS

1. Welding hazards are controlled by employing proper ventilation principles, using respirators and other personal protective devices including proper clothing, and by following safe working practices in general.

2. Proper methods for application of local mechanical exhaust ventilation or general dilution ventilation will vary with the type of welding being performed. In open-air welding or in large well-ventilated maintenance shops, the hazards from air-borne contaminants are not likely to be significant except for the more toxic fumes. For these highly toxic fumes and for heavy or production welding in a confined area, mechanical exhaust ventilation should be provided. Air supplied respirators or specifically designed local exhaust ventilation should be provided for welding on coated materials containing lead, cadmium, mercury, or other highly toxic materials. Local ventilation controls should be located as near to the welding operation as possible. When welding in confined areas, such as inside tanks or boilers, welders require a supplied air hood or air-supplied respirator.
3. Goggles or suitable eye protection should be worn during arc welding or cutting operations to provide protection from injurious rays and from flying objects. The helpers or attendants should also be provided with proper eye protection. Helmets, hand shields, and barriers around the operation provide for additional worker protection during the welding process.
4. Appropriate protective clothing required for any welding operation will vary with the size, nature, and location of work to be performed. Except when engaged in light work, all welders should wear flameproof gauntlet-style gloves. Flameproof aprons made of leather, asbestos, or other suitable materials may also be desirable as protection against radiated heat and sparks. Woolen clothing is preferable to cotton because it is not readily ignited and helps protect the welder from changes in temperature. Flame-resistant leggings, high boots, or other equivalent protection such as metal screens in front of the workers' legs should be used for heavy work. Ear protection may be required for work in extremely confined spaces, over-head welding, or plasma torch applications.

IV. MANAGEMENT RESPONSIBILITIES

Industrial management can help to prevent injuries to welders by informing them of the potential hazards and how to avoid them. Each supervisor has a definite responsibility to keep the workers in his area informed, to post warning signs, and to enforce safety protection measures. Local or general exhaust ventilation should be provided to control air contaminants as required by the various types of welding processes. Welding operations, when possible, should be isolated from other industrial operations, particularly degreasing tanks or solvent cleaning operations. Even with the level of trichloroethylene well below the maximum safe limit, there is the potential for dangerous concentrations of phosgene or other vapors to occur. Good housekeeping practices should be maintained throughout welding work areas.

V. RESPONSIBILITY OF WORKERS

Each worker should properly maintain and operate his welding equipment in such a manner as to avoid undue risk to health and safety. The following general rules and any others issued to protect him should be observed:
1. Abide by safety measures required for each type of welding.
2. Avoid electric shock.
3. Maintain equipment in good mechanical and electrical condition.
4. Be alert to possible fire hazards. Move the object to be welded to a safe location or remove flammable materials from the work area.
5. Utilize all required protective equipment and clothing.

6. Check the ventilation system before starting work and periodically thereafter to insure adequate performance.
7. Never weld inside drums or other confined spaces without adequate ventilation or the use of air-line respirators or self-contained breathing equipment.
8. Never weld in the same working area where degreasing or other cleaning operations are performed.
9. Cooperate with plant management in reporting defective equipment and hazardous working conditions.

GLOSSARY OF WELDING TERMS

TABLE OF CONTENTS

	Page
Air-Acetylene Welding ... Backup	1
Bare Electrode ... Carbon Electrode	2
Carbon-Electrode Arc Welding ... Cover Glass	3
Covered Electrode ... Electrode Force (Dynamic)	4
Electrode Force (Theoretical) ... Flux-Oxygen Cutting	5
Forehand Welding ... Helmet	6
Hold Time ... Interpass Temperature	7
Joint Brazing Procedure ... Metal-Arc Cutting	8
Metal Electrode ... Oxy-City Gas Cutting	9
Oxy-Hydrogen Cutting ... Platen Force	10
Plug Weld ... Push Welding	11
Quench Time ... Root of Weld	12
Root Opening ... Single-Bevel Groove Weld	13
Single-Impulse Welding ... Straight Polarity	14
Stress-Relief Heat Treatment ... Throat of a Fillet Weld	15
Throat of a Fillet Weld (Actual) ... Tical Position	16
Voltage Regulator ... Welding Goggles	17
Welding Ground ... Work Lead	18

GLOSSARY OF WELDING TERMS

A

AIR-ACETYLENE WELDING - A gas welding process wherein coalescence is produced by heating with a gas flame or flames obtained from the combustion of acetylene with air, without the application of pressure and with or without the use of filler metal.

ALL-WELD-METAL TEST SPECIMEN - A test specimen wherein the portion being tested is composed wholly of weld metal.

ARC CUTTING - A group of cutting processes wherein the severing of metals is effected by melting with the heat of an are between an electrode and the base metal.

ARC VOLTAGE - The voltage across the welding are.

ARC WELDING - A group of welding processes wherein coalescence is produced by heating with an electric arc or arcs, with or without the application of pressure and with or without the use of filler metal.

AS-WELDED - The condition of weld metal, welded joints and weldments after welding prior to any subsequent thermal or mechanical treatment.

ATOMIC-HYDROGEN WELDING - An arc-welding process wherein coalescence is produced by heating with an electric are maintained between two metal electrodes in an atmosphere of hydrogen. Shielding is obtained from the hydrogen. Pressure may or may not be used and filler metal may or may not be used.

AUTOMATIC OXYGEN CUTTING - Oxygen cutting with equipment which performs the cutting operation without constant observation and adjustment of the controls by an operator. The equipment may or may not perform loading and unloading of the work.

AUTOMATIC WELDING - Welding with equipment which performs the entire welding operation without constant observation and adjustment of the controls by an operator. The equipment may or may not perform the loading and unloading of the work.

AXIS OF A WELD - A line through the length of a weld, perpendicular to the cross-section at its center of gravity.

B

BACKFIRE - The momentary recession of the flame into the torch tip followed by an immediate reappearance or complete extinguishment of the flame.

BACKHAND WELDING - A gas-welding technique wherein the flame is directed opposite to the progress of welding.

BACKING - Material (metal, weld metal, asbestos, carbon, granular flux, etc.) backing up the joint during welding to facilitate obtaining a sound weld at the root.

BACKING PASS - A pass made to deposit a backing weld.

BACKING RING - Backing in the form of a ring generally used in the welding of piping.

BACKING STRIP - Backing in the form of a strip.

BACKING WELD - Backing in the form of a weld.

BACK PASS - A pass made to deposit a back weld.

BACK WELD - A weld deposited at the back of a single-groove weld.

BACKSTEP SEQUENCE - A longitudinal sequence wherein the weld bead increments are deposited in the direction opposite to the progress of welding the joint.

BACKUP - In flash and upset welding, a locator, used to transmit all or a portion of the upsetting force to the work pieces.

Bare Electrode -Carbon electrode

BARE ELECTRODE - A filler-metal electrode, used in are-welding, consisting of a metal wire with no coating other than that incidental to the drawing of the wire.

BARE METAL-ARC WELDING - An arc-welding process wherein, coalescence is produced by heating with an electric are between a bare or lightly coated metal electrode and the work arid no shielding is used. Pressure is not used and filler metal is obtained from the electrode.

BASE METAL - The metal to be welded or cut.

BASE METAL TEST SPECIMEN - A test specimen composed wholly of base metal.

BEAD WELD - A type of weld composed of one or more string or weave beads deposited on an unbroken surface.

BEVEL - A type of edge preparation.

BEVEL ANGLE - The angle formed between the prepared edge of a member and a plane perpendicular to the surface of the member.

BEVELING - A type of chamfering.

BLOCK BRAZING - A brazing process wherein coalescence is produced by heat obtained from heated blocks applied to the parts to be joined and by using a nonferrous filler metal having a melting point above 800°F but below that of the base metals. The material is distributed in the joint by capillary attraction.

BLOCK SEQUENCE - A combined longitudinal and build-up sequence for a continuous multiple-pass weld wherein separated lengths are completely or partially built up in cross-section before intervening lengths are deposited.

BOND - Junction of weld metal and base metal, or junction of base metal parts when weld metal is not present.

BOXING - Operation of continuing a fillet weld around a corner of a member as an extension of principal weld.

BRAZE - A weld wherein coalescence is produced by heating to suitable temperatures above 800F and by using a nonferrous filler metal, having a melting point below that of the base metals. Filler metal is distributed between closely fitted surfaces of joint by capillary attraction.

BUILD-UP SEQUENCE - Order in which weld beads of multiple pass weld are deposited with respect to cross-section of joint.

BUTT JOINT - Joint between two members lying approximately in the same plane.

BUTT WELD - Weld in butt joint.

BUTTON - In the destructive testing of spot-seam and projection-welded specimens, that part of a weld, including all or part of the nugget, which tears out.

C

CAPILLARY ATTRACTION - Phenomenon by which adhesion between the molten filler metal and the base metals together with surface tension of the molten filler metal, distribute the filler metal between the properly fitted surfaces of the joint.

CARBON-ARC CUTTING - An arc-cutting process wherein the severing of metals is effected by melting with the heat of an are between a carbon electrode and the base metal.

CARBON-ARC WELDING - An arc-welding process wherein coalescence is produced by heating with an electric are between a carbon electrode and the work and no shielding is used. Pressure may or may not be used and filler metal may or may not be used.

CARBON ELECTRODE - A non-filler-metal electrode, used In arc welding, consisting of a carbon or graphite rod.

CARBON-ELECTRODE ARC WELDING - A group of arc-welding processes wherein carbon electrodes are used.

CASCADE SEQUENCE - A combined longitudinal arid build-up sequence wherein weld beads are deposited in overlapping layer. (In manual shielded metal-electrode arc-welding, a backstep sequence is normally used.)

CHAIN INTERMITTENT FILLET WELDING - Two lines of intermittent fillet welding on a joint wherein the fillet weld increments in one line are approximately opposite to those in the other line.

CHAMFERING - The preparation of a contour, other than for a square groove weld, on the edge of a member for welding.

COLLAR - The reinforcing metal of a non-pressure thermit weld.

COMMUTATOR-CONTROLLED WELDING - The making of a number of spot or projection welds wherein several electrodes, in simultaneous contact with the work, progressively function under the control of an electrical commutating device.

COMPLETE FUSION - Fusion which has occurred over the entire base-metal surfaces exposed for welding.

COMPLETE JOINT PENETRATION - Joint penetration which extends completely through the joint.

COMPOSITE ELECTRODE - A filler-metal electrode, used in are welding, consisting of more than one metal component combined mechanically. It may or may not include materials which protect the molten metal from the atmosphere, improve the properties of the weld metal or stabilize the are.

COMPOSITE JOINT - A joint wherein welding is used in conjunction with a mechanical joining process.

CONCAVE FILLET WELD - A fillet weld having a concave face.

CONCAVITY - The maximum distance from the face of a concave fillet weld perpendicular to a line joining the toes.

CONCURRENT HEATING - The application of supplemental heat to a structure during a welding or cutting operation.

CONE - Conical part of a gas flame next to orifice of the tip.

CONTINUOUS SEQUENCE - A longitudinal sequence wherein each pass is made continuously from one end of joint to the other.

CONTINUOUS WELD - Extends without interruption for its entire length.

CONVEX FILLET WELD - A fillet weld having a convex face.

CONVEXITY - Maximum distance from face of convex fillet weld perpendicular to a line joining the toes.

COOL TIME - In multiple-impulse welding and seam welding, the time interval between successive heat times.

CORNER JOINT - Joint between two members located approximately at right angles to each other in form of an L.

CORONA - The area sometimes surrounding nugget of a spot weld at the faying surfaces which provides a degree of bonding.

COVER GLASS - Clear glass used in goggles, hand shields, and helmets to protect filter glass from spattering material.

COVERED ELECTRODE - Filler-metal electrode, used in arc welding, consisting of a metal core wire with a relatively thick covering which provides protection for the molten metal from the atmosphere, improves the properties of the weld metal and stabilizes the arc.
CRATER - Depression at termination of a weld bead.
CRATER CRACK - Crack in crater of a weld bead.
CROSS WIRE WELD - A projection weld made between crossed wires or bars.
CURRENT REGULATOR - Automatic electrical control device for maintaining constant current in primary of welding transformer.
CUTTING ATTACHMENT - Device attached to a gas-welding torch to convert it into an oxygen-cutting torch.
CUTTING TIP - That part of an oxygen-cutting torch from which the gases issue.
CUTTING TORCH - Device used in oxygen cutting for controlling and directing the gases used for preheating and the oxygen used for cutting the metal.

D

DEPOSITED METAL - Filler metal that has been added during a welding operation. DEPOSITION EFFICIENCY - Ratio of weight of deposited metal to net weight of electrodes consumed, exclusive of stubs.
DEPTH OF FUSION - The distance that fusion extends into base metal from surface melted during welding.
DIE - Resistance Welding - A member usually shaped to the work contour to clamp the parts being welded and conduct the welding current.
DIE - Fore Welding - Device used in forge welding primarily to form the work while hot and apply the necessary pressure.
DIE WELDING - Forge-welding process wherein coalescence is produced by heating in a furnace and applying pressure by means of dies.
DIP BRAZING - Brazing process wherein coalescence is produced by heating in a molten chemical or metal bath and by using a nonferrous filler metal, having a melting point above 800F but below that of the base metals. The filler metal is distributed in the joint by capillary attraction. When a metal bath is used, the bath provides the filler metal.
DOUBLE-BEVEL GROOVE WELD - Type of groove weld.
DOUBLE-J GROOVE WELD - Type of groove weld.
DOUBLE-U GROOVE WELD - Type of groove weld.
DOUBLE-VEE GROOVE WELD - Type of groove weld.
DRAG - Distance between point of exit of cutting oxygen stream and projection, on the exit surface, of point of entrance.

E

EDGE JOINT - Joint between edges of two or more parallel or nearly parallel members. EDGE PREPARATION - The contour prepared on edge of a member for welding. EFFECTIVE LENGTH OF WELD - Length of weld throughout which correctly proportioned cross-section exists.
ELECTRODE FORCE - Dynamic - In spot, seam and projection welding, the force (lbs.) between electrodes during actual welding cycle.

ELECTRODE FORCE - Theoretical - In spot, seam and projection welding, the force, neglecting friction and inertia, available at electrodes of a resistance welding machine by virtue of initial force application arid theoretical mechanical advantage of the system. ELECTRODE FORCE - Static - In spot, seam and projection welding, the force between electrodes under welding conditions, but with no current flowing and no movement in welding machine.

ELECTRODE HOLDER - Device used for mechanically holding electrode and conducting current to it.

ELECTRODE LEAD - Electrical conductor between source of arc-welding current and electrode holder.

ELECTRODE SKID - During spot, seam, or projection welding, the sliding of an electrode along surface of work.

ELECTRONIC HEAT CONTROL - Device for adjusting heating value (rms value) of current in making a resistance weld by controlling ignition or firing of tubes in an electronic contactor. Flow of current is initiated each half-cycle at an adjustable time with respect to zero point on voltage wave.

F

FACE OF WELD - Exposed surface of a weld, made by an arc- or gaswelding process, on the side from which welding was done.

FAYING SURFACE - That surface of a member in contact with another member to which it is to be joined.

FILLER METAL - Metal to be added in making a weld.

FILLET WELD - Weld of approximately triangular cross-section joining two surfaces approximately at right angles to each other in a lap, tee, or corner joint.

FILTER GLASS - Usually colored, used in goggles, helmets, and hand shields to exclude harmful light rays.

FLASH - Molten metal which is expelled or squeezed out by application of pressure, and solidifies around the weld.

FLASHBACK - Recession of flame into or back of mixing chamber of torch.

FLASHING TIME - In flash welding the time during which flashing action is taking place.

FLASH WELDING - Resistance-welding process wherein coalescence is produced, simultaneously over entire area of abutting surfaces, by heat obtained from resistance to flow of electric current between two surfaces, and by application of pressure after heating is substantially completed. Flashing and upsetting are accompanied by expulsion of metal from joint.

FLAT POSITION - Position of welding wherein welding is performed from upper side of joint and face of weld is approximately horizontal.

FLOW BRAZING - Brazing process wherein coalescence is produced by heating with molten nonferrous filler metal poured over joint until brazing temperature is attained. The filler metal has a melting point above 800F but below that of the base metals and is distributed in joint by capillary attraction.

FLOW WELDING - Welding process wherein coalescence is produced by heating with molten filler metal, poured over surfaces to be welded until welding temperature is attained and until required filler metal has been added. Filler metal is not distributed in joint by attraction.

FLUX - Fusible material used in welding or oxygen-cutting to dissolve and facilitate removal of oxides and other undesirable substances.

FLUX-OXYGEN CUTTING - An oxygen-cutting process wherein severing of metals is effected by using a flux to facilitate cutting.

FOREHAND WELDING - A gas-welding technique wherein the flame is directed toward progress of welding.

FORGE-DELAY TIME - In spot and projection welding, the time between beginning of weld time, or weld interval, and the time when electrode force first reaches the specified pressure for forging.

FORGE WELDING - A group of welding processes wherein coalescence is produced by heating in a forge or other furnace and by applying pressure or blows.

FULL FILLET WELD - A fillet weld whose size is equal to thickness of thinner member joined.

FURNACE BRAZING - A brazing process wherein coalescence is produced by heat obtained from a furnace and by using a non-ferrous filler metal, having a melting point above 800° F but below that of the base metals. Filler metal is distributed in joint by capillary attraction. FUSION - Melting together of filler metal and base metal, or of base metal only, which results in coalescence.

FUSION ZONE - Area of base metal melted as determined on crosssection of a weld.

G

GAS POCKET - Weld cavity caused by entrapped gas.

GAS WELDING - Group of welding processes wherein coalescence is produced by heating with gas flame or flames, with or without application of pressure, and with or without use of filler metal.

GROOVE - Opening provided for a groove weld.

GROOVE ANGLE - Total Included angle of groove between parts to be joined by a groove weld.

GROOVE FACE - That surface of a member included in the groove.

GROOVE RADIUS - Radius of a J- or U-Groove.

GROOVE WELD - Weld made in the groove between two members to be joined. The standard types of groove welds are as follows: Square Groove, Single-Vee Groove, Single-Bevel Groove, Single-U Groove, Single-J Groove, Double-Bevel Groove, Double-Vee Groove, Double-U Groove, Double-J Groove.

GROUND CONNECTION - Connection of work lead to work.

H

HAMMER WELDING - Forge-welding process wherein coalescence is produced by heating in a forge or other furnace and by applying pressure by means of hammer blows.

HAND-SHIELD - Protective device, used in arc welding, for shielding face and neck. A hand shield is equipped with a suitable filter glass and designed to be held by hand.

HEAT-AFFECTED ZONE - That portion of the base metal which has not been melted, but whose mechanical properties or microstructures have been altered by heat of welding or cutting.

HEAT TIME - In multiple impulse welding or seam welding, the time that current flows during any one impulse.

HEATING GATE - Opening in a thermit mold through which parts to be welded are preheated.

HELMET - Protective device, used in arc welding, for shielding face and neck. A helmet is equipped with a suitable filter glass and is designed to be worn on the head.

HOLD TIME - (1) In spot and projection welding, the time during which force is applied at point of welding after last impulse of current ceases to flow. (2) In seam, flash, and upset welding, the time during which force is applied to the work after current ceases to flow.

HORIZONTAL FIXED POSITION - Pipe Welding - The position of a pipe joint wherein the axis of the pipe is approximately horizontal and the pipe is not rotated during welding.

HORIZONTAL POSITION - Fillet Weld - The position of welding wherein welding is performed on the upper side of an approximately horizontal surface and against an approximately vertical surface.

HORIZONTAL POSITION - Groove Weld - The position of welding wherein the axis of the weld lies in an approximately horizontal plane and the face of the weld lies in an approximately vertical plane.

HORIZONTAL ROLLED POSITION - Pipe Welding - The position of a pipe joint wherein welding is performed in the flat position by rotating the pipe.

HORN - In resistance welding, a beam or arm, extending from frame of a welding machine which transmits electrode force and usually conducts welding current.

HORN SPACING - In a resistance-welding machine, the unobstructed work clearance between horns or platens at right angles to throat depth. This distance is measured with horns parallel and horizontal at the end of the downstroke.

HYDROGEN BRAZING - Method of furnace brazing in a hydrogen atmosphere.

I

IMPREGNATED-TAPE METAL-ARC WELDING - An arc-welding process wherein coalescence is produced by heating with an electric are between a metal electrode and the work. Shielding is obtained from decomposition of an impregnated tape wrapped around the electrode as it is fed to the arc. Pressure is not used and filler metal is obtained from the electrode.

INADEQUATE JOINT PENETRATION - Joint penetration which is less than that specified.

INCOMPLETE FUSION - Fusion which is less than complete.

INDENTATION - In a spot, seam, or projection weld, the depression on exterior surface(s) of base metal.

INDUCTION BRAZING - Process: wherein coalescence is produced by heat obtained from resistance of work to flow of induced electric current and by using a non-ferrous filler metal, having a melting point above $800°$ F but below that of the base metals. Filler metal is distributed in joint by capillary attraction.

INDUCTION WELDING - Process wherein coalescence is produced by heat obtained from resistance of work to flow of induced electric current, with or without pressure.

INERT-GAS CARBON-ARC WELDING - Process wherein coalescence is produced by heating with an electric arc between a carbon electrode and the work. Shielding is obtained from an inert gas such as helium or argon. Pressure and/or filler metal may or may not be used.

INTERMITTENT WELDING - Welding wherein continuity is broken by recurring unwelded spaces.

INTERPASS TEMPERATURE - In a multiple-pass weld, the lowest temperature of the deposited weld metal before next pass is started.

J

JOINT BRAZING PROCEDURE - Materials, detailed method and practices employed in brazing of a particular joint.
JOINT DESIGN - Joint geometry together with required dimensions of welded joint.
JOINT GEOMETRY - Shape and dimensions of a joint in cross-section prior to welding.
JOINT PENETRATION - Minimum depth a groove weld extends from its face into a joint, exclusive of reinforcement.
JOINT (UNWELDED) - Location where two or more members are to be joined by welding.
JOINT WELDING PROCEDURE - Materials, detailed methods and practices employed in welding of a particular joint.

K

KERF - The space from which metal has been removed by a cutting process.

L

LAP JOINT - Joint between two overlapping members.
LAYER - Stratum of weld metal, consisting of one or more weld beads.
LEAD BURNING - Misnomer for welding of lead.
LEG OF FILLET WELD - Distance from root of joint to toe of fillet weld.
LIGHTLY COATED ELECTRODE - A filler-metal electrode, used in are welding, consisting of a metal wire with a light coating applied subsequent to drawing operation, primarily for stabilizing the are.
LOCAL PREHEATING - Preheating a specific portion of a structure.
LOCAL STRESS-RELIEF HEAT TREATMENT - Stress-relief heat treatment of a specific portion of a structure.
LONGITUDINAL SEAM WELDING - Making of a seam weld in a direction essentially parallel to throat depth of a resistance welding machine.
LONGITUDINAL SEQUENCE - Order in which increments of a continuous weld are deposited with respect to its length.

M

MACHINE OXYGEN CUTTING - Oxygen cutting with equipment which performs cutting operation under constant observation and control of an operator. Equipment may or may not perform loading and unloading of the work.
MACHINE WELDING - Welding with- (same definition as above).
MANIFOLD - Multiple header for connecting several cylinders to one or more torch supply lines.
MANUAL OXYGEN CUTTING - Cutting wherein entire operation is performed and controlled by hand.
MANUAL WELDING - Entire operation performed and controlled by hand.
MASH SEAN WELD - Seam weld made in a lap joint wherein thickness of lap is reduced plastically to approximately the thickness of one of the lapped parts.
MELTING RATE - Weight or length of electrode melted in a unit of time.
METAL-ARC CUTTING - Process wherein severing of metals is effected by melting with heat of an are between a metal electrode and base metal.

Metal electrode-Oxy-city gas cutting

METAL ELECTRODE - Filler or non-filler-metal electrode, used in arc welding, consisting of a metal wire, with or without covering or coating.
METAL-ELECTRODE ARC WELDING - Group of arc-welding processes wherein metal electrodes are used.
MIXING CHAMBER - That part of a gas-welding or oxygen-cutting torch wherein the gases are mixed.
MULTIPLE-IMPULSE WELDING - Making of spot, projection and upset welds by more than one impulse of current. When alternating current is used, each impulse may consist of a fraction of a cycle(s).
MULTIPLE-IMPULSE WELD TIMER - In resistance welding, a device for multiple-impulse welding which controls only heat time, cool time, and either weld interval or number of heat times.

N

NEUTRAL FRAME - Gas flame wherein the portion used is neither oxidizing nor reducing.
NONPRESSURE THERMIT WELDING - Thermit-welding process wherein coalescence is produced by heating with superheated liquid metal resulting from chemical reaction between a metal oxide and aluminum without application of pressure. Filler metal is obtained from the liquid metal.
NONSYNCHRONOUS INITIATION - In resistance welding, the initiation or termination of welding transformer primary current at any random time with respect to voltage wave.
NUGGET - The weld metal joining the parts in spot, seam or projection welds.

O

OFF TIME - In resistance welding the time during which electrodes are off the work. This term is generally applied where the welding cycle is repetitive.
OPEN-CIRCUIT VOLTAGE - In arc welding, the voltage between terminals of a power source when no current is flowing in circuit.
OVERHEAD POSITION - Position of welding wherein welding is performed from underside of joint.
OVERLAP - Protrusion of weld metal beyond the bond at toe of weld.
OXIDIZING FLAME - Gas flame wherein the portion used has an oxidizing effect.
OXY-ACETYLENE - Process wherein severing of metals is effected by means of chemical reaction of oxygen with base metal at elevated temperatures, necessary temperature being maintained by means of gas flames obtained from combustion of acetylene with oxygen.
OXY-ACETYLENE WELDING - Gas welding process wherein coalescence is produced by heating with gas flame(s) obtained from combustion of acetylene with oxygen, with or without pressure and with or without use of filler metal.
OXY-ARC CUTTING - Oxygen-cutting process wherein severing of metals is effected by means of chemical reaction of oxygen with base metal at elevated temperatures, necessary temperature being maintained by means of an arc between an electrode and base metal.
OXY-CITY GAS CUTTING - Oxygen-cutting process wherein severing of metals is effected by means of chemical reaction of oxygen with base metal at elevated temperatures, necessary temperature being maintained by means of gas flames obtained from combustion of city gas with oxygen.

OXY-HYDROGEN CUTTING - Oxygen-cutting process wherein severing of metals is effected by means of chemical reaction of oxygen with base metal at elevated temperatures, necessary temperature being maintained by means of gas flames obtained from combustion of hydrogen with oxygen.

OXY-HYDROGEN WELDING - Gas welding process coalescence is produced by heating with gas flame(s) obtained from combustion of hydrogen with oxygen, without application of pressure and with or without use of filler metal.

OXY-NATURAL GAS CUTTING - Oxygen-cutting process wherein severing of metals is effected by means of chemical reaction of oxygen with base metal at elevated temperatures, necessary temperature being maintained by means of gas flames obtained from combustion of natural gas with oxygen.

OXY-PROPANE CUTTING - Oxygen-cutting process wherein severing of metals is effected by means of chemical reaction of oxygen with base metal at elevated temperatures, necessary temperature being maintained by means of gas flames obtained from combustion of propane with oxygen.

OXYGEN CUTTING - Group of cutting processes wherein severing of metals is effected by means of chemical reaction of oxygen with base metal at elevated temperatures. In the case of oxidation-resistant metals, reaction is facilitated by use of a flux. (See Cutting as follows: OXY-ACETYLENE, OXY-ARC, OXY-CITY GAS, OXY-HYDROGEN, OXY-NATURAL GAS, OXY-PROPANE, OXY-LANCE and FLUX-OXYGEN.)

OXYGEN-CUTTING OPERATOR - Operates machine or automatic oxygen-cutting equipment.

OXYGEN GOUGING - Application of oxygen cutting wherein a chamfer or groove is formed.

OXYGEN LANCE - Length of pipe used to convey oxygen to point of cutting in oxygen-lance cutting.

OXYGEN-LANCE CUTTING - Oxygen-cutting process wherein only oxygen is supplied by the lance and the preheat is obtained by other means.

P

PARTIAL JOINT PENETRATION - Joint penetration less than complete. PASS - A single longitudinal progression of a welding operation along a joint or weld deposit. Result of a pass 18 weld bead.

PEENING - Mechanical working of metals by hammer blows. PERCUSSION WELD - Made by percussion welding.

PERCUSSION WELDING - Resistance-welding process wherein coalescence is produced, simultaneously over entire area of abutting surfaces, by heat obtained from an arc produced by rapid discharge of stored electrical energy, with pressure percussively applied during or immediately following electrical discharge.

PLATEN - In a resistance-welding machine, a member with a substantially flat surface to which dies, fixtures, backups or electrode holders are attached, and which transmits electrode or upsetting force.

PLATEN FORCE - In flash and upset welding, the force available at the movable platen to cause upsetting. Force may be dynamic, theoretical or static.

Plug weld-Push welding

PLUG WELD - Circular weld made by either arc or gas welding through one member of a lap or tee joint joining that member to the other. Weld may or may not be made through a hole in first member. If a hole is used, the walls may or may not be parallel and hole may be partially or completely filled with weld metal. (A fillet-welded hole or a spot weld should not be construed as conforming to this definition.)

POKE WELD - See PUSH WELD.

POKE WELDING - See PUSH WELDING.

POROSITY - Gas pockets or voids in metal.

POSITIONED WELD - A weld made in a joint which has been so placed as to facilitate making the weld.

POSITION OF WELDING - See FLAT, HORIZONTAL, VERTICAL and OVERHEAD POSITIONS and HORIZONTAL ROLLER, HORIZONTAL FIXED and VERTICAL PIPE POSITIONS.

POSTHEATING - Application of heat to a weld or weldment subsequent to a welding or cutting operation.

POSTWELD INTERVAL - In resistance welding, the heat time between end of weld time, or weld interval, and start of hold time. During this interval the weld is subjected to mechanical and heat treatment.

PREHEATING - Application of heat to the base metal prior to a welding or cutting operation.

PRESSURE-CONTROLLED WELDING - Making of a number of spot or projection welds wherein several electrodes progressively function under control of a pressure-sequencing device.

PRESSURE GAS WELDING - Process wherein coalescence is produced, simultaneously over entire area of abutting surfaces, by heating with gas flames obtained from combustion of a fuel gas with oxygen and by application of pressure, without use of filler metal.

PRESSURE THERMIT WELDING - A thermit-welding process wherein coalescence is produced by heating with superheated liquid metal and slag resulting from the chemical reaction between iron oxide and aluminum, and by applying pressure. Liquid metal from the reaction is not used as filler metal.

PRESSURE WELDING - Any welding process or method wherein pressure is used to complete the weld.

PROGRESSIVE BLOCK SEQUENCE - Block sequence wherein successive blocks are completed progressively along the joint, either from one end to the other or from center of joint toward either end.

PROJECTION WELD - Weld made by projection welding.

PROJECTION WELDING - A resistance-welding process wherein coalescence is produced by heat obtained from resistance to flow of electric current through the work parts held together under pressure by electrodes. Resulting welds are localized at predetermined points by the design of the parts to be welded. The localization is usually, accomplished by projections, embossments or intersections.

PULSATION WELDING - See MULTIPLE-IMPULSE WELDING.

PULSATION WELD TIMER - See MULTIPLE-IMPULSE WELD TIMER.

PUSH WELD - A spot or projection weld made by push welding.

PUSH WELDING - The making of a spot or projection weld wherein the force is applied manually to one electrode and the work or a backing bar takes the place of the other electrode.

Q

QUENCH TIME - In resistance welding, that part of the postweld interval from cessation of flow of welding current -to-application of a current impulse for postheating.

R

RANDOM SEQUENCE - See WANDERING SEQUENCE.
RATE OF DEPOSITION - See DEPOSITION RATE.
RATE OF PLANE PROPAGATION - Speed at which a flame travels, through a mixture of gases.
REACTION STRESS - Residual stress which could not otherwise exist if the members or parts being welded were isolated as free bodies without connection to other parts of the structure.
REACTOR - Device used in arc-welding circuits for purpose of minimizing irregularities in flow of welding current.
REDUCING FLAME - Gas flame wherein the portion used has a reducing effect.
REGULATOR - Device for controlling delivery of gas at some substantially constant pressure regardless of variation in the higher pressure at the source.
REINFORCEMENT OF WELD - Weld metal on the face of a groove weld in excess of metal necessary for the specified weld size.
RESIDUAL STRESS - Stress remaining in a structure or member as a result of thermal or mechanical treatment or both.
RESISTANCE BRAZING - Process wherein coalescence is produced by heat obtained from resistance to flow of electric current in a circuit of which the work is a part and by using a non-ferrous filler metal, having a melting point above 800° F, but below that of the base metals. The filler metal is distributed in joint by capillary attraction.
RESISTANCE BUTT WELDING - See UPSET WELD-FLASH WELD.
RESISTANCE BUTTING WELDING - See UPSET WELDING and FLASH WELDING.
RESISTANCE WELDING - A group of welding processes wherein coalescence is produced by heat obtained from resistance of work to flow of electric current in a circuit of which the work is a part, and by application of pressure.
RESISTANCE WELDING ELECTRODE - See ELECTRODE.
REVERSE POLARITY - The arrangement of direct current arc-welding leads wherein the work is the negative pole and the electrode is the positive pole and the electrode is the positive pole of the welding arc.
ROLL SPOT WELDING - Making of separated spot welds with circular electrodes.
ROLL WELDING - A forge-welding process wherein coalescence Is produced by heating in a furnace and by applying pressure by means of rolls.
ROOT - See ROOT OF JOINT arid ROOT OF WELD.
ROOT CRACK - A crack in the weld or base metal occurring at the root of a weld.
ROOT EDGE - A root face of zero width. See ROOT FACE.
ROOT FACE - That portion of the groove face adjacent to the root of the joint.
ROOT GAP - See ROOT OPENING.
ROOT OF JOINT - That portion of a joint to be welded where members approach closest to each other. In cross-section the root of the joint may be either a point, line or an area.
ROOT OF WELD - The points, as shown in cross-section, at which the bottom of the weld intersects the base metal surfaces.

Root opening-Single-bevel groove weld

ROOT OPENING - The separation between the members to be joined, at the root of the joint.
ROOT PENETRATION - Depth a groove weld extends into the root of a joint measured on the centerline of the
ROOT RADIUS - See GROOVE RADIUS.

S

SCARF - See EDGE PREPARATION.
SCARFING - See CHAMFERING.
SEAL WELD - Any weld used primarily to obtain tightness.
SEAM WELD - A weld consisting of a series of overlapping spot welds, made by seam or spot welding.
SEAM WELD TIMER - In seam welding, a device which controls heat times and cool times.

Seam Welding -Spacer Strip

SEAM WELDING - Resistance-welding process wherein coalescence is produced by heat obtained from resistance to flow of electric current through work parts held together under pressure by circular electrodes. Resulting weld is a series of overlapping spot welds made progressively along a joint by rotating the electrodes.
SELECTIVE BLOCK SEQUENCE - Block sequence wherein successive blocks are completed in a certain order selected to create a predetermined stress pattern.
SEMIAUTOMATIC ARC WELDING - Arc welding with equipment which controls only filler metal feed. Advance of the welding is manually controlled.
SERIES WELDING - Making of two spot or seam welds or two or more projection welds simultaneously with three electrodes forming a series circuit.
SEQUENCE TIMER - In resistance welding, a device for controlling sequence and duration of any or all of the elements of a complete welding cycle, except weld time or heat time.
SEQUENCE WELD TIMER - In resistance welding, a device for controlling sequence and duration of any or all of the elements of a complete welding cycle.
SHEET SEPARATION - In spot, seam, arid projection welding, the gap surrounding the weld, between faying surfaces, after joint has been welded.
SHIELDED CARBON-ARC WELDING - An arc-welding process wherein coalescence is produced by heating with an electric are between a carbon electrode and the work. Shielding is obtained from combustion of a solid material fed into the are or from a blanket of flux on the work or both. Pressure may or may not be used and filler metal may or may not be used.
SHIELDED METAL-ARC WELDING - Arc-welding process wherein coalescence is produced by heating electrode and the work. Shielding is obtained from decomposition of electrode covering. Pressure is not used and filler metal is obtained from the electrode.
SHIELDED STUD WELDING - Arc-welding process wherein coalescence is produced by heating with an electric are drawn between a metal-stud, or similar part, and the other work part, until surfaces to be joined are properly heated, when they are brought together under pressure. Shielding is obtained from an inert gas such as helium or argon.
SHOULDER - See ROOT FACE.
SHRINKAGE STRESS - See RESIDUAL STRESS.
SINGLE-BEVEL GROOVE WELD - A type of groove weld.

SINGLE-IMPULSE WELDING - The making of spot projection and upset weld by a single impulse of current. When alternating current is used, an impulse may consist of a fraction of a cycle or a number of cycles.

SINGLE-J GROOVE WELD - A type of groove weld.

SINGLE-U GROOVE WELD - A type of groove weld.

SINGLE-VEE GROOVE WELD - A type of groove weld.

SIZE OF WELD - Groove Weld - The joint penetration (depth of chamfering plus the root penetration when specified).

SIZE OF WELD - Fillet Weld - For equal length of the largest isosceles right-triangle which can be inscribed within the filletweld cross-section. For unequal leg fillet welds, the leg lengths of the largest right-triangle which can be inscribed within the fillet-weld cross-section.

SKIP SEQUENCE - See WANDERING SEQUENCE.

SLAG INCLUSION - Nonmetallic solid material entrapped in weld metal or between weld metal and base metal.

SLOT WELD - Weld made in an elongated hole in one member of a lap or tee joint joining that member to that portion of surface of other member which is exposed through the hole. The hole may be open at one end and may be partially or completely filled with weld metal. (A fillet-welded slot should not be construed as conforming to this definition.)

SLUGGING - Act of adding a separate piece or pieces of material in a joint before or during welding resulting in a welded joint which does not comply with design, drawing or specification requirements.

SPACER STRIP - Metal strip or bar inserted in the root of a joint prepared for a groove weld, to serve as a backing and maintain root opening during welding.

SPATTER - In arc and gas welding, the metal particles expelled during welding and which do not form a part of the weld.

SPATTER LOSS - Metal lost due to spatter.

SPIT - See FLASH.

SPOT WELD - A weld made by spot welding.

SPOT WELDING - A resistance-welding process wherein coalescence is produced by the heat obtained from resistance to the flow of electric current through the work parts held together under pressure by electrodes. The size and shape of the individually formed welds are limited primarily by the size and contour of the electrodes.

SQUARE GROOVE WELD - A type of groove weld.

SQUEEZE TIME - In spot, seam projection and upset welding, the time interval between the initial application of the electrode force on the work and the first application of current.

STACK CUTTING - Oxygen cutting of stacked metal plates arranged so that all the plates are severed by a single cut.

STAGGERED INTERMITTENT FILLET WELDING - Two lines of intermittent fillet welding on a joint wherein the fillet weld increments in one line are staggered with respect to those In the other line.

STATIC ELECTRODE FORCE - See ELECTRODE FORCE.

STEPBACK SEQUENCE - See BACKSTOP SEQUENCE.

STORED ENERGY WELDING - The making of a weld with electrical energy accumulated electrostatically, electromagnetically or electrochemically at a relatively low rate and made available at the required welding rate.

STRAIGHT POLARITY - The arrangement of direct current arc-welding leads wherein the work is the positive pole and the electrode is the negative pole of the welding arc.

STRESS-RELIEF HEAT TREATMENT - Uniform heating of a structure or portion thereof to a sufficient temperature, below the critical range, to relieve the major portion of the residual stresses, followed by uniform cooling. (Note: Terms normalizing, annealing, etc., are misnomers for this application.)
STRING BEAD - A type of weld bead made without appreciable transverse oscillation.
STRING BEADING - Deposition of string beads.
STUD WELDING - Arc-welding process wherein coalescence is produced by heating with an electric are drawn between a metal stud, or similar part, and the other work part until the surfaces to be joined are properly heated, when they are brought together under pressure, and no shielding is used.
SUBMERGED ARC WELDING - Arc-welding process wherein coalescence is produced by heating with an electric are or arcs between a bare metal electrode or electrodes and the work. The welding is shielded by a blanket of granular, fusible material on the work. Pressure is not used and filler metal is obtained from the electrode and sometimes from a supplementary welding rod.
SURFACING - Deposition of filler metal on a metal surface to obtain desired properties or dimensions.
SYNCHRONOUS INITIATION - In spot, seam, and projection welding, the initiation and termination of each half-cycle of welding-transformer primary current so that all half-cycles of such current are identical.
SYNCHRONOUS TIMING - See SYNCHRONOUS INITIATION.

T

TACK WELD - Weld made to hold parts of a weldment in proper alignment until the final welds are made.
TEE JOINT - Joint between two members located approximately at right angles to each other in the form of a T.
TEMPER TIME - In resistance welding, that part of the postweld interval during which a current suitable for tempering or heat treatment flows. The current can be single or multiple impulse, with varying heat and cool intervals.
THEORETICAL ELECTRODE FORCE - See ELECTRODE FORCE.
THERMIT CRUCIBLE - The vessel in which the thermit reaction takes place.
THERMIT MIXTURE - A mixture of metal oxide and finely divided aluminum with the addition of alloying metals as required.
THERMIT MOLD - A mold formed around the parts to be welded to receive the molten metal.
THERMIT REACTION - The chemical reaction between metal oxide and aluminum which produces superheated molten metal and aluminum oxide slag.
THERMIT WELDING - A group of welding processes wherein coalescence is produced by heating with superheated liquid metal and slag resulting from a chemical reaction between a metal oxide and aluminum, with or without the application of pressure. Filler metal, when used, is obtained from the liquid metal.
THROAT DEPTH - In a resistance-welding machine, the distance from the center-line of the electrodes or platens to the nearest point of interference for flatwork or sheets. In the case of a seamwelding machine with a universal head, the throat depth is measured with the machine arranged for transverse welding.
THROAT OF A FILLET WELD - Theoretical - The distance from the beginning of the root of the joint perpendicular to the hypotenuse of the largest right-triangle that can be inscribed within the fillet-weld cross section.

THROAT OF A FILLET WELD - Actual - The shortest distance from the root of a fillet weld to its face.
THROAT OPENING - See HORN SPACING.
TIP SKID - See ELECTRODE SKID.
TOE CRACK - A crack in the base metal occurring at the toe of a weld.
TOE OF WELD - The junction between the face of a weld and the base metal.
TORCH - See WELDING TORCH or CUTTING TORCH.
TORCH BRAZING - A brazing process wherein coalescence is produced by heating with a gas flame and by using a non-ferrous filler metal having a melting point above 800° F, but below that of the base metal. The filler metal is distributed in the joint by capillary attraction.
TORCH TIP - See WELDING TIP or CUTTING TIP.
TRANSVERSE SEAM WELDING - The making of a seam weld in a direction essentially at right angles to the throat depth of a seam-welding machine.
TUNGSTEN ELECTRODE - A nonfiller-metal electrode, used in arc welding, consisting of a tungsten wire.
TWIN-CARBON-ARC BRAZING - A brazing process wherein coalescence is produced by heating with an electric arc maintained between two carbon electrodes and by using a non-ferrous filler metal, having a melting point above 800F, but below that of the base metals. The filler metal is distributed in the joint by capillary attraction.
TWIN-CARBON-ARC WELDING - An arc-welding process wherein coalescence is produced by heating with an electric arc maintained between two carbon electrodes and no shielding is used. Pressure is not used and filler metal may or may not be used.

U

ULTRA-SPEED WELDING - See COMMUTATOR-CONTROLLED WELDING.
UNDERBEAD CRACK - A crack in the heat-affected zone not extending to the surface of the base metal.
UNDERCUT - A groove melted into the base metal adjacent to the toe of a weld and left unfilled by weld metal.
UPSET - The localized increase in volume in the region of a weld, resulting from the application of pressure.
UPSET BUTT WELDING - See UPSET WELDING.
UPSET WELD - A weld made by upset welding.
UPSET WELDING - A resistance-welding process wherein coalescence is produced, simultaneously over entire area of abutting surfaces' or progressively along a joint, by the heat obtained from resistance to the flow of electric current through the area of contact of those surfaces. Pressure is applied before heating is started and is maintained throughout the heating period.
UPSETTING FORCE - In flash and upset welding, the force exerted at the welding surfaces during upsetting.
UPSETTING TIME - In flash and upset welding, the time during upsetting.

V

VERTICAL POSITION - Position of welding wherein axis of weld is approximately vertical. VERTICAL POSITION - Pipe Welding - Position of a pipe joint wherein welding is performed in horizontal position and pipe may or may not be rotated.

VOLTAGE REGULATOR - Automatic electrical control device for maintaining constant voltage supply to primary of a welding transformer.

W

WANDERING BLOCK SEQUENCE - A block sequence wherein successive blocks are completed at random after several starting blocks have been completed.
WANDERING SEQUENCE - A longitudinal sequence wherein weld bead increments are deposited at random.
WAX PATTERN - Wax molded around the parts to be welded by a thermit welding process, to the form desired for the completed weld.
WEAVE BEAD - Type of weld bead made with transverse oscillation.
WEAVE BEADING - Deposition of weave beads.
WELD - A localized coalescence of metal wherein coalescence is produced by heating to suitable temperatures, with or without application of pressure, and with or without use of filler metal. Filler metal either has a melting point approximately the same as base metals or has a melting point below that of the base metals but above 800° F.
WELDABILITY - Capacity of a metal to be welded under fabrication conditions imposed into a specific, suitably designed structure and to perform satisfactorily in the intended service.
WELD BEAD - Weld deposit resulting from a pass. See STRING AND WEAVE BEAD.
WELD CRACK - A crack in weld metal.
WELD DELAY TIME - In spot and projection welding, the time that weld time is delayed to insure proper sequence of mechanical functions in relation to subsequent electrical functions.
WELD GAGE - Device for checking shape and size of welds.

WELD INTERVAL - In resistance welding, the total of all heat and cool times when making a single, multiple-Impulse weld.
WELD INTERVAL TIMER - In resistance welding, a device which controls heat and cool times and weld interval when making multiple-impulse welds singly or simultaneously.
WELD LINE - See BOND.
WELD METAL - Portion of a weld melted during welding.
WELD METAL AREA - Area of weld metal as measured on cross-section of weld.
WELD PENETRATION - See JOINT PENETRATION and ROOT PENETRATION.
WELD TIME - In single-impulse welding and flash welding, the time that welding current is applied to the work in making a weld.
WELD TIMER - In resistance welding, a device controlling only weld time.
WELDED JOINT - Union of two or more members produced by application of a welding process.
WELDER - One capable of performing a manual or semi-automatic welding operation.
WELDING CURRENT - Current flowing through welding circuit during the making of a weld. In resistance welding, the current used during preweld or postweld intervals is excluded.
WELDING CYCLE - In resistance welding, the complete series of events involved in the making of a weld.
WELDING ELECTRODE - See ELECTRODE.
WELDING FORCE - See ELECTRODE and PLATEN FORCE.
WELDING GENERATOR - Supplies current for welding.
WELDING GOGGLES - Goggles with tinted lenses which protect eyes from harmful radiation and damage from flying particles.

WELDING GROUND - See WORK LEAD.

WELDING LEADS - The work lead and electrode lead of an arc-welding circuit.

WELDING PRESSURE - The pressure exerted during the welding operation on the parts being welded. (See also ELECTRODE FORCE and PLATEN FORCE.)

WELDING PROCEDURE - The detailed methods and practices including joint welding procedures involved in the production of a weldment.

WELDING PROCESS - A metal-joining process wherein coalescence is produced by heating to suitable temperatures, with or without the application of pressure, and with or without the use of filler metal. (See FORGE WELDING, THERMIT WELDING, FLOW WELDING, GAS WELDING, ARC WELDING, RESISTANCE WELDING, INDUCTION WELDING, and BRAZING.)

WELDING ROD - Filler metal, in wire or rod form, used in gas welding and brazing processes, and those arc-welding processes wherein the electrode does not furnish the filler metal.

WELDING SEQUENCE - The order of making the welds in a weldment.

WELDING TECHNIQUE - The details of a manual, machine or semi-automatic welding operation which, within the limitations of the prescribed joint welding procedure, are controlled by the welder or welding operator.

WELDING TIP - A welding torch tip designed for welding.

WELDING TORCH - A device used in gas welding or torch brazing for mixing and controlling the flow of gases.

WELDING TRANSFORMER - A transformer used for supplying current for welding.

WELDING WHEEL - See ELECTRODE.

WELDMENT - An assembly whose component parts are joined by welding.

WELDOR - See WELDER.

WORK LEAD - The electric conductor between the source of arc-welding current and the work.

www.ingramcontent.com/pod-product-compliance
Lightning Source LLC
Chambersburg PA
CBHW082209300426
44117CB00016B/2738